Nagme, Kisse, Baatein, Yaadein

The life & lyrics of Anand Bakshi

RAKESH ANAND BAKSHI

EBURY
PRESS

An imprint of Penguin Random House

EBURY PRESS

USA | Canada | UK | Ireland | Australia
New Zealand | India | South Africa | China

Ebury Press is part of the Penguin Random House group of companies
whose addresses can be found at global.penguinrandomhouse.com

Published by Penguin Random House India Pvt. Ltd
7th Floor, Infinity Tower C, DLF Cyber City,
Gurgaon 122 002, Haryana, India

First published in Ebury Press by Penguin Random House India 2021

ISBN 9780670094950

Typeset in Adobe Jenson Pro by Manipal Technologies Limited, Manipal
Printed at Replika Press Pvt. Ltd, India

www.penguin.co.in

'Woh hote hain kismatwale, jinki maa hoti hai'

—Anand Prakash Bakhshi

To our mother, to his Maaji, and to his fans and listeners

—Bakshis, Datts, Balis, Soods and Mehras

Contents

Foreword by Salim Khan   ix

A Note by the Family   xiii

Woh Tadbeerien Nahin Hotin   xv

Introduction   xvii

Prologue   xxi

1. 1930–1944: Happiness Is Born   1
2. 1944–1947: 'Jo Nahi Batt Saki Cheez Woh Reh Gayi'   15
3. 1947–1950: 'My Aim in Life'   25
4. 1950–1951: 'Yahan Main Ajnabi Hoon'   38
5. 1951–1956: A Daughter Gives Birth to a Father and Lyricist   44
6. 1956–1959: 'Zindagi Har Qadam Ek Nayi Jung Hai'   55
7. 1959–1967: Inking His Way to the Top   68
8. A Being of Divine Light and Power   95
9. 'Mushkil Mein Hai Kaun Kissi Ka'   124
10. 2000–2002: 'The Best News Is That I Am Alive'   134

Tributes   151

Epilogue   170

What's a Legend?   178

Highlights of Anand Bakshi's Career (1956–2002)   182

The Relevance of Anand Bakshi Today   188

Acknowledgements   195

Foreword by Salim Khan

When a child is born in India, the parents not only give him an appropriate name according to his star sign but also get his destiny chart prepared by an astrologer. This is no ordinary custom, as it could be an image and reflection of a lifetime. Some people who believe in superstitions select weak or inappropriate names for their children. I have known some rich people who gave their children names that mean the opposite of their actual financial status and character; and I also know of poor people who gave their children names that signify immense wealth. But some people prove in their lifetime that they were rightly named.

A child born in a tiny village in Punjab was named Anand (happiness) Bakshi (to gift) by his parents, and all his life this poet gifted happiness to millions of his listeners. He was gifted with the talent of writing poetry that enthralled people throughout his professional span of more than fifty years in a life that lasted seventy-two years. Very few people are as fortunate and as gifted to be able to fulfil their destiny on earth with such flair and style as the late Anand Bakshi.

Around the time of Indian Independence, very few socialist poets wrote film songs, like Josh Malihabadi, Sahir Ludhianvi, Kaifi Azmi, Shailendra. The poets of that period were imbued with the colours of Indian nationalism. And they were politically coloured too, the effect of which we heard in their film songs. There's nothing wrong in being attached to the politics of the state or believing in a particular ideology. Every poet has a right to his or her beliefs and convictions. All these above-mentioned poets have written wonderful songs. Yet Anand Bakshi was never influenced by or attached to any socialist or political ideologies. He was first and foremost a film songwriter who was completely immersed in, just as his writings emerged from, the characters and the narrative of the film he was working on. He didn't have and aspire for fame in the world of poetry, but he was among the very best in the world of film songs. His success in writing film songs could make one feel that he took birth only to fulfil his destiny of being one of the best lyricists.

In that period, there already were great established poets around—like Shailendra, Raja Mehdi Ali Khan, Prem Dhawan and others. There was no opportunity, and no one could stand against these giants, especially a meagre soldier with poetic ambitions. The many famous music composers of that time already had their favourite poets and songwriters they were happy working with; so there was no scope of Anand Bakshi breaking through, especially with other good poets, like Indeevar and Anjaan, waiting in the wings much before Anand Bakshi arrived on the scene with his pen and paper. But it was his courage that made Anand Bakshi jump straight into the fiery sea of competition where much bigger fish already ruled the waves.

Anand Bakshi had a great sense of humour and musical acumen, and he even had the gift of capturing and expressing deep philosophical ideas using few and simple words. Slowly but gradually, he began to receive work to write film songs. When Anand Bakshi was knocking on the doors of success, there appeared on the horizon the rising sun of Laxmikant–Pyarelal. The musical duo and geniuses recognized the talent in Anand Bakshi, and soon made him their favourite and preferred lyricist. The triangle of Anand Bakshi, Laxmikant and Pyarelal rewrote the history of Hindi film songs, with nearly 303 films they did together. He also made a great pair with R.D. Burman: ninety-nine films.

Bakshi was a very simple, unpretentious and sincere man. He had a phobia of air travel and of enclosed lifts of high-rise buildings (the claustrophobic lifts made him fear having to meet workmates or friends who worked or lived in high-rises). But he climbed high on the steps of life and reached the pinnacle of success, passing every step on the strength of his talents. He was not one who would have used any sort of machine other than his own talent to rise high in this world.

It was the culture of his village in Punjab that beat in his simple heart. That's why he never found himself lost in the mega dream city of Bombay, nor was he ever affected by the fact that the path to his dreams was but a jungle of illusions and obstacles. His simplicity and humility was his strength that kept his head above water, even when he tasted success consistently, year after year.

His humility was also the very bridge that helped him cross over— from his urban and NRI fan base—into the hearts of the people of the heartland, his rural listeners. He forged ties with both the hearts and the minds of his listeners all over, by using simple and everyday words carrying the deepest philosophical meanings. His simplicity was so sincere that he would often invite himself to my home by saying, 'Because you live on the first floor, and one does not need to travel by lift to reach your home, and since your beloved wife Salma cooks the most delicious meals, I am coming over for a meal at your home tonight.'

In show business, I have experienced that most celebrities and people hide their true intentions; their hearts don't reflect what they say. But Bakshi wasn't like that—he was unique in this sense. He achieved much fame through his writing, which he earned via his life's varied experiences. He firmly believed that at every moment life is offering you lessons, but because we are preoccupied with our material and physical goals, overwhelmed by our ambitions and challenges, we are unable to absorb the valuable lessons life offers us alongside.

We have cut short the antennae that help us pick up these signals and lessons of life, and thus we do not recognize the teachings of Mother Nature. Life's lessons are imprinted in the very grains of sand that we leave our footprints on, but sadly we blind ourselves to them.

This lesson that Bakshi taught me reminds me of an incident from a film I wrote, *Naam*. The protagonist in my story has migrated to a foreign land to earn a better living for his family. But he gets trapped in the illusion of ambitions. He suddenly remembers his mother, and now he badly misses the love of his family back home. Bakshi understood the pain and suffering of this protagonist so well, and he expressed himself in a most popular song, on the strength of which the film did a roaring business. The song was, '*Chitthi aayee hai watan se chitthi aayee hai* (A letter from home has arrived, a memory of love has arrived).'

When he was on his deathbed in the hospital, Bakshi wrote a song for Subhash Ghai for a yet-to-release film entitled *Majnu*. I was awestruck by the depth of the lyrics when I heard them. It also amazed me that he wrote the song in illness, just before death arrived knocking at his door. I believe he wrote because writing was not only his religion but his breath, his mission for the cycle of life and death, much beyond his destiny.

There have been many poets who were much better than him, but he was supreme among the songwriters. He passed away on 30 March 2002, having written, since 1957, more than 650 films and 3500 film songs. He wrote songs for every occasion and relationship of life, even though he could never manage to complete his schooling. Bakshi was a star. He became a legend. And legends never die. He lives on in his songs and in our hearts.

A Note by the Family

This book about our father, lyricist Anand Bakshi, is seeing the light of day after nineteen years of his passing. My siblings, Rajesh and Kavita, and I are very thankful to Rakesh for his consistent and remarkable efforts in putting our daddy's life's journey on paper with the help of memories, expressions and impressions of many of his and our father's friends, relatives and associates.

This is the story of our father's struggles till and after he became a significant part of the film world, which he'd dreamt of since he was a teenager, sitting on the pavement outside their house in Rawalpindi, entertaining friends by singing the songs and verses he'd heard on the radio, seen in films and written himself. He not only worked at fulfilling his dream; he also saw to his family's needs and comforts through thick and thin. He *always* kept us, and the stories of the films he had been writing lyrics for, in sharp focus in his mind. He ensured that his children and wife, Kamla, his biggest supporter, had the guidance and financial support they needed while he tried to make a name for himself, and he worked even harder to live up to the success he was able to achieve. He would say that in the film profession it's even harder to live up to your success than it is to become successful. He credited his God, his family and his luck and for his success, never himself.

Rakesh writes about our daddy Anand Bakshi's life with passion, tenderness and reverence, tracing his evolution quite intimately at times. From how he achieved the optimum level of creativity as a poet and lyricist to how he was as the family man we knew, Rakesh looks back on it all, with the assistance of some unbelievable documents preserved by our father through the decades, from the time he was in school! He never considered himself a poet, and that's exactly why I am making it a point to mention here—if he can listen to me and his fans—that he was one!

As I read through the chapters on his formative years, his challenges, his early years of success, to the point when he was finally hailed by Subhash Ghai as the uncrowned king of lyricists on his sixty-eighth birthday, I relived in flashback his entire life.

The book attempts to trace the life of this inimitable figure, whose depiction of every aspect of human relations through his simple words and simpler metaphors made even a common man easily understand and identify with his lyrics. His ambition was to be writing till his last breath; he wanted to 'die with my boots on', which he did. He wrote approximately 3000–3500 songs, until about three weeks before his passing, on 30 March 2002. He is much missed by not just his family, friends and associates but also his fans worldwide. He and his work cannot be forgotten for a long time, which is proven by the many recreations and remixes of his songs even in the latest movies today.

Our daddy was and is our hero.

March 2021   Suman Vinay Datt (daughter)
Mumbai

Woh Tadbeerien Nahin Hotin[*]

Jo tadbeeron se phir jaaein woh taqdeerein nahin hotin
Badal dein jo na taqdeerein woh tadbeerein nahin hotin

Mohabbat ke mahal ka toh tassavvur bhi nahin asaan
Wafa ke taj ki aasaan taamirein nahin hotin

Rihaai ka musammam azam (ahed) kar letey hain jab qaidi
Toh kaaraamad sitamgaaron ki zanjeerein nahin hotin

Mohabbat ka taalluq rooh se makhsoos hota hai
Yeh dil ki baat hai aur iss pe taqreerein nahin hotin

Samajh bhi lein mohabbat ko toh hum samjah nahin saktey
Kitab-e-ishq ki lafzon mein tafseerein nahin hotin

---

* This is the first poem Anand Bakshi wrote to inspire himself sometime in 1956, when he made his second attempt at trying his luck in Bombay ('Bambai,' as he would say) as a song writer, leaving the army the second time for his dream. The essence of this poem is that if your destiny (taqdeerein) can be changed by your deeds/actions (tadbeerein), then it's not really your 'destiny'; it's not destined (taqdeer) for you. And, if your deeds/actions can't change your destiny, then they aren't really 'deeds/actions'.

Khuloos aur sadqe ke sajdon mein taseerein jo hotin hain
Dikhawe ki ibadat mein woh taseer nahin hotin

Khud unki deed se Bakhshi tassavur unka behtar hai
Ke itni bemurawwat unn ki tasveerein nahin hotin

Introduction

Aadmi Musafir Hai

'*Aadmi musafir hai, aata hai jaata hai, aate jaate, raste mein yaadein chhod jaata hai*'

—From the film *Apnapan*

I was first encouraged to write a biography of my father, the late Anand Bakshi, by his fans, my family, close friends and my first publisher Shantanu Ray Chaudhuri way back in 2012. I had told Shantanu then that I had been putting one together since 2002 and had about 150 pages, which I could send him only after I had a published book or a film to my name. This was because Dad had told me, 'Don't do anything in my name after I am gone until you first have something of your own in this world.' It took me fifty years to create something of my own—my first book as an author, *Directors' Diaries: The Road to Their First Film*, was published in 2015. Only after that did I begin to seek a publisher for this biography, which is seeing the light of day finally, thanks to Penguin Random House.

I began to think of what I had been writing since 2002 in earnest as a 'book' only about seven or eight years ago. Prior to that, I felt I was too close to my father to write about him, and that the book may come across as a form of hero worship. But I was wrong. The biggest reward of writing this book is that it brought me closer to my siblings; I stopped taking them for granted, because while writing this book I began to remember and realize that the four of us were the top priority for Mom and Dad, and not his songs. While he was around, I had sometimes felt his songs were more important than us, which distanced me from the daddy I had adored as a kid and teen. I was proved wrong as I further researched and wrote this book. Over the last decade of writing this book, I fell back in love with my daddy.

While working on the book I also realized that my family's true inheritance is not just our daddy's inspiring, entertaining and pertinent songs, which many of his fans constantly remind me of now and then, or his fame; our inheritance is also what was taken away from him and his family, and from millions of others, by the politics that led to the partition of the Indian subcontinent in 1947. Moreover, our true inheritance is his resilience and grit, his *hausla* in building a life not just for himself alone but for his family too, always keeping us in sight like he kept the tip of his pen and the pages of his lyrics and personal diaries. Much of the intimate information in this book is thanks to his meticulously written personal diaries.

However, before we go back in time, and to the birth of Nand, Anand Bakshi's nickname, I would like to say that I am neither an expert on Hindi film songs nor on Anand Bakshi's songs. I am just a son writing a book about his daddy's journey, whatever little I know of his life's path and have learnt through his lyrics. I am also not privy to every event mentioned in this book and have gathered some of these from the hundreds of his fans I have met over the years. The book also includes what I've heard over four decades from Dad, and from our family and relatives. Much of the text in the first person comes from the notes I have taken from dad's journals/diaries because I want to give an authentic flavour to the memoir and make it sound as close to his voice as possible.

So I look forward to suggestions from you readers, fans, journalists who have featured him or his work—people who know his songs or perhaps some anecdotes connected to them that I am not aware of and could not include in this book. We will work on your suggestions to improve on this edition and will share your valuable suggestions in the book's next edition. This is our first attempt at doing justice to Anand Bakshi.

One of the biggest lessons I learnt writing this book, other than valuing my family more, is that even if you have only one person in this world who believes in you, you can achieve your dream, your goal, your ambition—even if that one person is yourself.

A big lesson my brother Gogi and I learnt from Dad as children was that we always had to be fair and not cheat, whatever the situation or circumstance. Yes, your dreams matter, and it is important to do what you do for your livelihood. You may or may not succeed at it. But what will matter the most, especially when you arrive closer to the silver or golden period of your life, is the kind of human being you have become, succeeding at things or failing at them.

Stay inspired. *Shukriya, khushaamadeed*, happy reading.

Prologue

It was 2 October 1947, a date that is now celebrated as Gandhi Jayanti. The subcontinent had been divided a few weeks ago by the arbitrary and infamous Radcliffe Line, compelling millions to flee as refugees overnight, many penniless and hopeless, with what they could grab before they were killed or raped or burnt. Prakash Vaid Bakhshi—he was fondly called Nand by his Maaji, and Azeez by his Papaji—was among them.

He was seventeen at that time, and his family was living in Pindi, (Rawalpindi), now in Pakistan. The Bakhshi *khaandaan* had to flee overnight the security of an ancestral home for a life of humiliation, loss of dignity, emotional and financial uncertainty and insecurity, and what could have been possibly the ultimate loss—that of life. Eleven years earlier, Nand had suffered an even bigger and irreparable loss: the loss of his mother, Mitra, whom he called Maaji. She die when Nand was six years 'young', due to pregnancy-related complications.

The Bakhshi family travelled safely from Pindi to Delhi via a Dakota airplane; they were 'safe' because my Dad's Bauji (grandfather) was the superintendent of police, Punjab Jails, Lahore and Rawalpindi. Before the joint family hurriedly embarked on their journey across the border, his family—consisting of his half-siblings, stepmother, Papaji and paternal grandparents, Bauji and Biji—had to grab, within minutes, whatever money, clothes and personal belongings they could possibly carry with them on the army-supplied secure truck and on the Dakota airplane. The elders had received a tip-off that same day that their mohalla was going to be attacked by rioters and marauders any minute.

The suddenly displaced and distressed family (now labelled by circumstance as 'refugees') reached Delhi the next day. They were received by Nand's Bauji's sister Vanti's son, and they stayed with this family at Dev Nagar for a few hours and then went to Poona (Pune) for refugee registration. Once the family had settled down, got hold of their emotions, senses and scarce personal belongings, Dad's Bauji and Papaji asked all the elders what they had carried across the border. Bauji asked the seventeen-year-old Nand what he had managed to grab before embarking on the military truck. Dad said that he had carried family photographs. On learning this, he received a loud scolding from the family elders: 'What useless things have you carried with you! How will we survive without valuables?'

Nand replied: '*Paise toh hum naukri kar ke kamaa sakte hain, magar Maa ki tasveer main kahan se laoonga, agar woh peeche rehe jaati? Mujhe toh Maa ka chehera bhi yaad nahi. Inn tasveeron ke sahare hi main aaj tak jeete aaya hoon.* (Money can be earned by working. But had I left Mother's photograph behind, where would I have got it from? I don't even remember Mother's face. These photos are what I have lived on).'

Even as a seventeen-year-old, and in the middle of chaos at home with impending riots in their mohalla, Nand had the sensibility that made him think of his late Maaji's photographs as the most precious item to carry across the border.

1

1930–1944

Happiness Is Born

Geetkaar Anand Bakshi was born in undivided India, on 21 July 1930 at 7.55 a.m. He was Daddy for us children, Nand for his Maaji, Mitra (Sumitra), Azeez or Azeezi for his Papaji, and Nando for relatives.

The Bakhshis resided in a three-storey house in Chittian Hattian, Mohallah Qutubuddin, Rawalpindi—a house that stands even today. Their house was famously known as 'Daroga Ji Ka Ghar' or 'Daroga Ji Ki Kothi', because his Bauji was a superintendent of police during the British Raj.

'There was a water well, a gurdwara, a masjid and a Hindu school in the neighbourhood. I would eat the "kadha" prasad (wheat sweet) at the gurdwara, sing along with the Gurbani Shabad kirtan, drink water from the well and whistle to the melodic azan from the masjid on my way home from school. I would know the time of the day from the azan and the sound of the Lord Krishna mandir's bells near our house. It was a secular and happy neighborhood.

'I would leave my bicycle, one among a handful in our village, at any place in our neighbourhood and return home. Some neighbours would always return it by evening when they found it abandoned. Many people in our village knew Daroga Ji Ki Kothi—"*Yeh toh Daroga ji ke pote ki cycle hai.*"'

1

The Bakhshi khaandaan lived as a joint family, consisting of Nand's Bauji, Bakhshi Sughar Mall Vaid, deputy superintendent of police, Punjab Jails, stationed in Pindi; Biji (paternal grandmother); Papaji (father), Bakhshi Mohan Lal Vaid; and Maaji (mother), Sumitra Bali Bakhshi.

'Our home back in Pindi was extremely organized, orderly and disciplined due to Bauji being in the police service and Papaji being a bank manager. Bauji would wear a white pagri made of thin 'mulmul' (cotton) cloth, starched firm, just like he was, with a straw *kula*, a kind of cone at the top. My years in the Royal Indian Navy and the fauj later cemented my organized mind. It is only an organized mind that can create good work.'

Nand's Maaji expired from an illness during her pregnancy, or perhaps during childbirth, when she was twenty-five years old. In a correspondence between Dad and his maternal uncle Major W.M. Bali, his Maaji's brother mentions, '. . . Nand, I know you have suffered psychologically, being brought up motherless and sent away from home at a very early age . . .'

After Nand's mother departed, he preferred to be with Biji rather than with his father. Back then, Bauji was posted in Lahore for some years, in charge of the women's jail. Nand, motherless, accompanied him so he could spend time with his Biji. 'Her love came quite close to a mother's.' Nand's Papaji soon remarried. Yashoda Devi Bali became his second wife. She was Nand's late mother Sumitra's first cousin. Nand continued to miss his Maaji even after having achieved fame and success, and having had four children of his own. He would speak of his formative years in Pindi and his Maaji like it was a shattered dream.

I was told by Dad's Maasi, Mrs Nirmal Mehta Chhibber, 'Your daddy's Maaji was fondly addressed as Mitri or Mitra by her family. She was playful and musically inclined. She sang Punjabi songs beautifully. She would dress up as a male, always played the male-actor roles in drama performances staged during family weddings.' In retrospect, his Maaji's fondness for singing and performing drama must have certainly penetrated little Nand's subconscious mind—he was an impressionable child. He was the first and only child of his mother, Sumitra.

Biji began to address him as Nand after his Maaji's death in 1936. (Earlier he was her Nando.) She raised Nand like a mother since he was six years old.

'Biji would comb my hair gently with a wooden comb. Her buttermilk and home-made white ghee on thick wheat *baasi* (stale) parathas was my favourite treat before I ran out to play on the streets after school hours. *Gajar da halwa* and *aate da halwa* (the way they prepare it in gurdwaras) were among her specialties that I loved. On some days, she would secretly pack it in my school lunch to surprise and delight me. Though she loved me like my own mother, I still wished my mother was around.'

'*Maa Khuda toh nahi. Lekin Maa, tu Khuda se kam bhi nahi* (Mother, you're not God, but you're no less than God),' Dad would say in praise of his Maaji and later of the mother of his own children.

Decades later, when he was serving in the Indian Army and had his own first child, a daughter, in 1956, for him it was a sign of good luck from God. Because Biji had told him, '*Betiyan, piyoh de liye achcha naseeb laandi hain* (Daughters bring good luck for their fathers).' His daughter's birth became the catalyst for him to leave the army and take the plunge into 'trying his luck' in films a second time.

Biji would also say the best way to love your children is to love their mother. When I would sometimes be rude to my Mom, Dad would tell me, 'You are rude to her because you have a mother. So you don't value her. I lost mine when I was six. Ask me the value of one. I thirst for her embrace, have felt so ever since.'

* * *

'*Chitthi na koi sandesh, jaane woh kaun sa desh, jahan tum chale gaye*'
—*Dushman*

Anand Bakshi wrote innumerable memorable lyrics in praise of the mother's love. Perhaps more than any other lyricist. Many of his songs—in films like *Khal Nayak* ('Maa Tujhe Salaam'), *Chhota Bhai* ('Maa Mujhe Apne Aanchal Mein Chhupa Le'), *Raja Aur Runk* ('Tu Kitni Achhi Hai' and 'Mere Raja Mere Lal Tujhko Dhoondoon Main Kahan'), *Aasra, Maa, Mastana* ('Maine Maa Ko Dekha Hai Maa Ka Pyar Nahin Dekha'), and *Amar Prem* ('Bada Nathkhat Hai Re'), among others—have some of the finest lyrics on the mother–child relationship.

* * *

'Baatein, bhool jaati hain, yaadein, yaad aati hain. Yeh yaadein, kissi, dil-o-janam ke, chale jaane ke baad aati hain. Yaadein, meethi meethi yaadein'
—*Yaadein*

Nand's Papaji had six children with his second wife, Yashoda Devi: Uma, Shubh, Indira, Jeevan, Ashok and Ved. Shubh and her husband, the late Khem Raj Dutt, had an affectionate relationship with Dad. In the 1970s, Dad assisted one of his stepbrothers in his college graduation and provided financially for his Papaji until he passed away in 1974 in Delhi. His half siblings loved him, yet Dad missed having siblings from his own Maaji.

Nand enrolled in an Urdu-medium school, Cambridge College, Rawalpindi. After that, he joined the Royal Indian Navy and subsequently signed up for the Indian Army as 'Anand Prakash'. When Anand Prakash first began writing poems as a *fauji* during his first posting in the army, around 1947–50, he signed them as Anand Prakash Bakhshi. He came to be addressed as 'Anand Bakshi' only 1959 onwards, after the release of his first film, *Bhala Admi*, because 'Bakshi', even 'Baxi', was how his family name was mistakenly mentioned in the film credit titles. Eventually, 'Bakshi' stuck for good.

The elders—Papaji, Bauji and, later, Dad's father-in-law, Amar Singh Mohan—addressed him as 'Azeez', the most loved one, in their written correspondence, particularly in the letters where they scolded him severely for leaving a secure job like the army (with the family not even having a house of their own post-Partition) for an uncertain life and profession in an alien city like Bambai. 'I belonged to an ancestry of policemen, faujis and zamindars, but I was the black sheep of my family!'

In their martial community of Mohyals, who are said to have originated from northern India, the 'film profession' was considered lowly.

* * *

'Mere desh mein, pawan chale, purvai . . .'

Sometime in 1988, Anand Bakshi was once asked by a friend when and how he had developed his skills as a lyricist. This is what he said:

'My love for film songs began with my passion to sing and play the banjo. Lyrics writing cannot be taught. With time, you can polish this skill. However, the talent, what they term creativity today, has to be inborn. In retrospect, my development as a writer and singer began in my childhood in Pindi. *Mera gaon, meri maa, meri mitti thi wo* (It was my village, my mother, my soil). I loved to sing film songs and play the banjo. I would effortlessly write dialogues and verses for the Ram Leela, Sohni–Mahiwal, Laila–Majnu *nautankis*/dramas, that were held regularly in our neighbourhood on festive occasions. I would sing the verses I wrote on the street outside my house and even perform them on stage. You would not be given good roles back then unless you could sing too. The dramas of Agha Kashmiri and Munshi Premchand were modern and liked very much; the fables, Laila–Majnu, Heer–Ranjha, Shireen–Farhad, Sohni–Mahiwal, attracted hundreds. I played roles in nearly all of them. Actor, director and producer Sunil Dutt was my Mohyal relative, and we would together sing and perform dramas during weddings in our close-knit community. *"Suhe ve cheere waleya main kehni aan"* was a very popular wedding song I loved to sing and dance to. Performing as women was common as few Punjabi girls dared to act or sing.

'We would go to the Pindi market with friends to buy fresh sugarcane and shred it with our teeth, without using a knife—we felt some macho pride in being able to do that. A man selling *patte wali* (leaf) ice cream would arrive daily in our lane, ringing a bell to announce his arrival and carrying a *taraazu* for weight measurement. Camels would walk through town on market days, and it was a fascinating sight for us kids to see. We would follow them till we reached a mohalla we were not familiar with. The dice game was called charter, and it was our favourite pastime post-school and before reaching home. We would bathe in a friend's field on the outskirts of Pindi, with water drawn from a well using oxen. Stealing fruits from strangers' trees was our favourite pastime and *chori ke* (stolen) fruits always tasted the best.

'In cities today, we do not know our immediate neighbours' names. When I was a child, we knew our whole mohalla. And everyone knew us. Papaji and Bauji would beat me with a stick whenever someone told them they saw me watching or performing a play. Bauji's beatings with his walking stick were so severe that I shudder with pain remembering them even today. They became even stricter with me after Maaji passed away as they feared that a motherless child would go wayward very easily. They would call me a *kanjar*—it's the name of a nomadic tribe but was sometimes used as a derogatory word back then for film and theatre artists. Films and theatre were strictly discouraged in our household, though we had a gramophone and Papaji liked to listen to devotional and Saigal's songs. We Mohyals were meant to belong to the armed forces, to banking; we were meant to be professionals. Naukri pesha. Running a business was also not considered. "*Humare khoon mein nahi hai* (It's not in our blood)."

'I loved MUSIC! Musically recited Ramayana and Gita, the Guru Granth Sahib paths and the melodic azan were heard throughout the day in our neighbourhood. I loved hearing the farmers singing in their fields when they were sowing or harvesting or entertaining themselves after sunset. Maybe that is why I could write something like "*Mere desh mein pawan chale, purvai*" or "*Likha hai yeh inn hawaon mein, likha hai yeh in ghataon mein, main hoon tere liye, tu hai mere liye*" effortlessly.

'The simple sounds of everyday village life, nature, folk music, everything about Punjab fascinated me. I loved listening to the radio and the devotional songs played on Papaji's gramophone. Mukesh, Lata, Mohammed Rafi were my inspirations too. I was very fond of singing Saigal's songs on stage. I would attend all weddings, sometimes uninvited, in my village, just to hear the music played there and sing. My mind simply went on absorbing every sound, smell and colour in my neighbourhood, my natural environment for seventeen years. I never realized this then, but my family environment, not having a mother, and my surroundings shaped my very sensitive and very emotional temperament. I have also paid a price for this, as I feel hurt very easily.'

* * *

'*Mere geeton mein meri kahaniyan hain, kaliyon ka bachpan hai, phoolon ki jawaniyan hain*'

—*Teri Kasam*

'Everybody is musical. We talk, walk, write in certain rhythms depending on the time, mood, need. Our heart has a rhythm, our breath too; even our relationships—every relationship has a different rhythm, we don't behave the same with every person. We share some common rhythms with acquaintances, some with a close friend, with a beloved. I do not believe anyone is born without music and rhythm. It is just that some lose touch with the chords in them, and some turn deaf to the same for whatever reasons.

'I experienced harvest festivals, celebrated festivals of all religions, attended melas, slept under moonlight. We would gather around winter fire to chat, sing, dance. I was addicted to the radio as a child. I liked to watch movies that had action and magic. I would sell my school books to see films. I never missed a film of John Cawas, Nadia and action films. I loved to sing and play the banjo. I would entertain my friends by singing film songs, Punjabi folk numbers and ghazals.

'In hindsight, I had the knowledge of metre in songwriting right from my teens. I was already writing parodies of popular songs and my own one- to two-sentence *nazms* (poems) then. Right from my school days, I desired to be a singer and actor in films, though I was clueless what it meant to be one or if it could be a career or source of livelihood. It seemed fun, that's it, and it got me a lot of attention in our extended family and among friends. Bauji was the one who hated it the most, so I never performed if he was around. When I joined the army in 1947, I somehow knew that one day my songs will play on the radio, though I did not know how to achieve that, so I dreamt of going to Bombay and doing something in films; I just wasn't clear exactly what.

'My first poem got published when I was a teen, in a Pindi newspaper called *Qaumi*. I did not think too much of this, though I was very excited and showed it off to friends only. If Maaji had been alive, I would have shown her, and she would have loved it. I wanted to be only a singer in films, not a songwriter, as I was not aware how one wrote songs in films. After my matriculation, I even travelled to the Lahore film industry to find work as a singer and actor. Bauji was posted there, so I had a house, and I missed Biji and wanted to spend time with her. She was the only one who understood me.

'It was during my early years in the fauj, in 1947, that I began to write poetry in earnest. By then, I had become aware of the names of the people who'd written the songs I sang, and I also came to know what music composer and film producer meant. I would compose my poems in metre as songs and sing them to my soldier mates and seniors in the barracks. Appreciation from my seniors in particular made me feel I had a talent. Gradually, I began to perform songs at our annual theatre events, the Bara Khanas. Bara Khanas were organized throughout the army on national days, both in peace and field areas.

'Singing songs and composing my own verses as a child kindled the flame of poetry and music in me. My childhood experiences held me in good stead and enriched my lyrics decades later. It was my aim in life, from around 1950, to leave the fauj and become an "artist". It was a highly respected word back then among people who appreciated films and songs, *ki yeh ek "artist" hai; inn logon ki kuch aur hi tabiyat hoti hai* (that he is an "artist"; these people have a different temperament). I began to read even more about such "artists" in the Urdu and Hindi features I could lay my hands on during my weekly breaks from the cantonment in the various towns I got posted in.'

* * *

'Padhai se jaan chhooti'

Anand Prakash (that was the name he was enrolled under) studied at the Urdu-medium Cambridge College. Hindi was never the language he read or wrote in regularly. He was more comfortable writing in and reading English and Urdu. A decade later, when he began to write poems during his army years, he always wrote in the Urdu script. This practice continued when he began writing lyrics for films. He had to always narrate them to his directors and composers, and they would note them down in Hindi or Roman Hindi scripts.

He was often complimented for writing so effectively using simple, everyday Hindi words and asked about the secret behind his 'genius'. In a 2001 interview, he told journalist Devmani Pandey, 'I was educated only till class nine. I did not have a large Hindi vocabulary. I had no choice but to use the few words I had to say what I needed to express. My limited vocabulary seems to have perhaps held me in good stead; it worked in my favour as a film song lyricist. It is the reason behind my success, as most people could understand and even sing these songs.'

That's him underplaying his skills, I believe. It's anything but easy to incorporate simple truths in conversational sentences. Quoting just

one verse from his 3300-plus songs, and among my favourite classics,
'Kuch Toh Log Kahenge' (*Amar Prem*), '. . . *Tu kaun hai, tera naam
hai kya, Sita bhi yahan, badnaam hui*.'

* * *

'*Chalo, singer bante hain*'

When Anand Prakash, the teenager, first dreamt of being in films, it
was to become a singer and not a lyricist.

'After my matriculation in Pindi, sometime in 1943, I made a visit
to Lahore under the pretext of being with my beloved Biji. Bauji was
posted there, in charge of the Lahore Women's Jail. I went around
Lahore trying to find the building where films are made. I thought
the site would be located in one building, where they all get together
and sing songs and make these films. I could not make any headway in
Lahore. I was dejected, but I still kept hoping, thinking it's better I go
to Bambai and try my luck there.'

'*Kahe ko roye, chaahe jo hoye, safal hogi teri Aradhana*'

—*Aradhana*

* * *

'*My trip to nowhere*'

Not one to give up easily on his dream, Anand Prakash made another
attempt soon, this time to reach faraway 'Bambai'.

'My two friends from Pindi, who used to perform in theatre, and I
planned to run away from home and go to Bambai by train to find work
in films. None of us got any support from home. We promised each
other we would stay together and STRUGGLE together. We gave each
other himmat (confidence) as all three of us were very high on ideals.

'To seal our bond of friendship and ambition to "struggle" together in Bambai, we tattooed each other's names on our forearms! With the plan in place, I even sold my school books and reached the Rawalpindi railway station so we could embark on our train journey to the land of our dreams. I waited all day for my friends. However, they never showed up. I did not have the courage to leave for an alien faraway land all alone. I was just 13–14 then. Once again, my dream crushed, I returned home before sunset.

'Naturally, soon enough Papaji and Bauji discovered that I had sold off all my books, and I received a solid thrashing from Bauji. It was worse than the thrashing he'd given me when he saw me acting on stage. One of our community elders had found out I was performing and had led Bauji to the spot. I had to leave the play midway and run home to Papaji.

'Soon, sometime in 1943, I was packed off to a boarding school in Jammu, a gurukul—far from the "distractions" of Pindi, according to the elders of my family. They felt that staying far away from my "Pindi de kanjar dost", who were initiating me in singing and acting, would make a "gentry" out of me. I was heartbroken leaving Pindi and Biji, and felt the absence of my Maaji even more now. Had my own Maaji been alive then, she would never have let them do this to me. Biji was powerless in our home. I had to move on.'

'Aaj ka yeh din, kal ban jayega yeh kal, peeche mudh ke na dekh, pyare aage chal'

—Nastik

* * *

'I don't want free milk!'

'Within a few days of the first term beginning, I enrolled for boxing classes at my gurukul, only because they gave boxers one glass of milk free to drink daily. The boxing teacher, our sports teacher, had a cruel way of teaching us. Every day, he would randomly select one student and beat him until the student fell unconscious. Somehow, I managed to escape his keen eye for selecting students to beat to a pulp daily. I cleverly stayed out of his way and enjoyed the daily glass of milk without having to wear boxing gloves.

'After many months of enjoying the free milk, successfully keeping out of his sight, *one day* he noticed me! "Oye! You are someone I have never noticed before. Have you just joined school? No? Okay! Wear your gloves. I will teach you how to defend like a man!" He beat me till I fell to the ground. That was the last day I craved for free milk. If we refused to be part of the sadistic ritual of being beaten to pulp by him, we had to become *murga* (putting arms under legs, squatting and holding our ears in the squat position) out in the sun until we collapsed with fatigue. It was worse than my previous school, where our headmaster would hold a naughty student by both ears and lift him off the floor. Soon enough, in the middle of the term, I ran away from the gurukul and returned to Pindi on my own. I was given the thrashing of my life for abandoning my higher studies.'

Papaji and Bauji feared Nand will again get involved in theatre if he remained in Pindi and decided to enlist him as a naval cadet in the Royal Indian Navy, Karachi, lest he became a wastrel. Moreover, the martial community of Mohyals took pride in being part of the armed forces. So it was about time their Azeez *puttar* lived up to his ancestry.

Nand was more than happy to leave home this time. Karachi was not as far from Lahore or Rawalpindi as Jammu was, and he could meet his Papaji and Biji more often. When he was enrolled at the gurukul by his Bauji and some other elders, I think he felt abandoned by his family. He felt they had distanced him 'emotionally', left him 'alone' among strangers. This fear of abandonment or anxiety of being alone was to emerge later as one of his lifelong phobias that gradually began to show itself in the '70s and would overwhelm him from the mid-'90s onwards.

Nand felt he was not receiving the kind of affection he expected or should have received from his Papaji and stepmother. He would stay out of the house for most of the daylight hours and return only by dusk, before Bauji and Papaji returned home. In my opinion, this was probably one of the main factors that made him willing to enlist in the navy, besides the biggest motivator: the training ship he was to be posted on was docked at Karachi. In his young head he put two and two together. Karachi harbour would become his route to reach the film industry in Bambai!

This was his second and perhaps the final chance to make another attempt at trying his luck in Bombay. So he was eager to sign up.

Even though Nand had been unhappy with the manner he felt he was brought up by his Papaji after the demise of his Maaji, he fulfilled his duty towards the family when he attained fame and fortune. Here is a letter from his cousin that says Anand Bakshi tried his best to save his Papaji's life when the latter was suffering from health problems in Delhi and finally succumbed to them.

There was this person at his childhood home who was unhappy with Nand's presence and would beat him with a belt buckle in order to get rid of him. Then, this person would inflict self-harm, with a leather belt, and go around showing the injury marks to the family elders, claiming that Nand, the wastrel, had done this. This was the darkest period of Nand's childhood and teenage years. He suspected that this person did this to him to drive him away from his home and family. I do not know why he was beaten up like this and falsely implicated for hurting another family member. But, because the elders believed that family member, Nand would often get a scolding or beating as the punishment for a crime he had not committed in the first place.

Now, I do not know how it feels to lose your mother at the age of six. My mom lived a full life with us. I don't know whether a child as sensitive as Nand, whose Maaji departed so early and whose father remarried soon after, needed extraordinary attention and affection. Dad never went into the details; he said it hurt him to talk about those years. He would often speak to us about the loss of his Maaji and the loss of his land of birth, Pindi—his two big losses. 'No amount of fame and money and affection thereafter was able to replace both, *meri* Maaji *aur meri mitti* (land). *Meri mitti thi, Jhelum mein woh behe gayi* (My land got washed away into the Jhelum).'

* * *

'*Kitab-e-gham mein khushi ka koi fasana dhoondo, agar jeena hai zamane mein toh khushi ka koi bahana dhoondo. Shayana woh hai jo pathjhad mein bhi bana le gulshan baharon jaisa, kagaz ke phoolon ko bhi jo meheka kar dikhalaye. Ik banjara gaye.*

—*Jeene Ki Raah*

At fourteen years of age, Anand Prakash was enrolled in the Royal Indian Navy, Karachi Harbour, in the year 1944, with the intention to serve the nation in the armed forces. The elders expected him to live up to their Mohyal ancestry. However, destiny (taqdeer) and Nand's actions and deeds (tadbeer) were to prove otherwise.

'*Taqdeer hai kya, main kya jaanu, main aashiq hoon tadbeeron ka*'

—*Vidhaata*

* * *

The first published poem of Anand Bakhshi, when he was a teenager in Pindi:

Aye Khuda, gham teri duniya ke main pee sakta nahin
Mangta hoon aaj kuch, ab honth see sakta nahin.
Zindagi! is waaste jeene ko bhi karta hai dil
Aur maut! is khatir ke mein aur jee sakta nahin.
Haan, is gulshan pe aayi hain bahaarein lakh baar
Haan, isi wadi pe barsi hai ghataein baar baar.
Aaj jo basti tujhe dikhti hai registaan si
Hum nasheen, ek din yahin se phoote the, aabshaar.

2

1944–1947

'Jo Nahi Batt Saki Cheez Woh Reh Gayi'

Nand was enlisted as Anand Prakash—rank 'Boy 1' (rating)*—on board the HMIS *Dilawar* in Karachi on 12 July 1944, and he continued to serve there till 4 April 1945, after which he was transferred to HMIS *Bahadur*.

'On the very first day itself, we were sent to an in-house barber for the military-pattern haircut—sides chopped off and faint traces of hair just at the top. A typical day would begin at 0400 hours, and we would get thirty minutes to get ready and put on the uniform. At 0445 hours we would assemble for vigorous physical training exercises. Our studies would begin at 0900 hours and last till lunch, at noon. Lunchtime was thirty minutes. Our classes finished at 1400 hours. At 1500 hours, we had to take up some kind of sports activity on the ground, and our studies would begin again at 1800 hours and go on till 2100 hours. Dinner was thirty minutes till 1930 hours. We would hit the bed and fall asleep in minutes. One enjoyed the taste of the food at the mess, but eventually, with time, that taste would fade

---

* Rating is a junior enlisted member who is not a warrant or commissioned officer. HMIS *Bahadur* was the Boys' training establishment on shore in Manora, a small peninsula located south of the Port of Karachi.

away, and then one hated the place, dying to go onshore on the next day of leave and gorge on the food available at the local stalls. The sea sailing would start only after three years, for which we had to undergo special training. I had assumed I will soon be on my way to Bambai, the land of my film dreams!'

The months went by as the trainee and cadet Anand Prakash hoped against hope that his ship would sail to the Bombay harbour someday soon. However, both the ships that he enlisted on, from 1944 to 1946, never left the Karachi harbour! His ambition to reach Bombay via the 'navy route' was not materializing. However, something far more dramatic was in store for him. He got enmeshed in the naval mutiny! It had originated from Calcutta and had quickly spread to the Bombay and Karachi harbours by February 1946.

* * *

Bagaawat: The Indian Naval Mutiny

While he was on board one of the two ships, Anand Prakash found himself in the midst of a naval mutiny: his peers and seniors had decided to revolt against the British officers.

According to what my dad recounted on the balcony of our Bandra house one evening, over his favourite Red Label drink and we kids sipping our Coca Cola a family routine when we were kids:

'The mutineers were led by a fiery Bengali boy. My ship was soon taken charge of by a British commanding officer, A.C. Moore, and his force. The commanding officer on board my ship asked the Bengali boy on board the adjacent ship to surrender. I wanted to be on the other ship, siding with my peers. I decided to hoodwink the British officer to join the mutineers on their ship. I thought we would be able to overpower the British force employed to crush the mutiny. Hundreds of Indian sailors and officers were shouting "Jai Hind" and azaadi (freedom) slogans, and the atmosphere was charged, nationalist and patriotic.

'I told our British commanding officer, "Sir, I know the Bengali boy. He is my good friend. I can convince him to surrender. If you will allow me to disembark and board his ship." The commanding officer, perhaps convinced by my young age or "innocent" looks, allowed me to board the ship of the mutineers. Once I got on the mutineers' ship, I joined my peers in slogan-shouting against the British Raj. I had always thought it humiliating to be ruled by a foreign power. And with my extended family in the armed forces, I would sometimes hear them talk about the freedom struggle going around in Bombay, Delhi, Calcutta and other places. I had not joined the navy to fight for my country; I had joined to make my way to the Bombay harbour. However, at that moment I forgot everything and wanted to be a part of what was far bigger than anything I had experienced! Patriotism awakened in me only after I joined the navy. Bauji and our family had always hated being "ruled" by outsiders. Suddenly, I wanted to be like them!

'However, our *josh* was shot down mercilessly. The naval mutiny was crushed soon, and we arrested mutineers were paraded in front of the same British commanding officer A.C. Moore, whom I had hoodwinked. Surprisingly, he recognized me. He found out I was fifteen years old. He told me, "You are too young for me to arrest and punish in a jail. If I do, which I can indeed, your life will be over perhaps. I will not do that, but I will dismiss you from the service."'

Anand Prakash was dismissed from the Royal Indian Navy on 5 April 1946, within two months of the mutiny.

As the *Heritage Times* reported, 'About forty ratings of HMIS *Bahadur* proceeded to the quarter deck, pulled down and tore the Ensign, hoisting in its pace a "Jai Hind" flag. They made their way to HMIS Chamak, the Radar Training School. However, when they tried to enter, the boys from Chamak resisted, but gave in after a while. The crowd then proceeded to HMIS Himalaya, which was similarly invaded ... When the mutiny ended in Karachi on 23 February 1946, eight lives had been lost and 33 persons lay wounded, including some British soldiers.*

'In retrospect, when I think about that day after so many years, I cannot thank officers A.C. Moore and Davis Wilfred John Williams— if I recollect correctly, both were in charge of us boy ratings—enough for their wisdom and graciousness in not punishing an underage naval cadet. Because he was responsible for my second chance at life. Who knows if I would have died in jail or survived. But I do feel now that had he jailed me, my life would have taken a very different course and I would perhaps have never reached Bambai and become a geetkar.'

In 1983, Anand Bakshi, pushed by the relatives who had proudly served the armed forces, applied for status as freedom fighter, but the Ministry of Home Affairs rejected his proposal in 1986, for 'lack of proof' of him being one of the mutineers.

* * *

'*Main film pe film dekhta tha*'

Back in Pindi, instead of lamenting the past failure, he looked forward to his passion, of somehow remaining close to his dream: films.

In 1946, after his dismissal from the navy, Nand took up a job at a cinema in Rawalpindi as a ticket booking clerk, so that he could watch movies for free. I have no idea what his Bauji's plans for him were for his higher education or career. If I recollect correctly, he worked at Rose Cinema, Rawalpindi. I don't know how he managed to keep this job a secret from his family.

'Songs and action scenes were what fascinated me about films to begin with. Story began to appeal to me post my teens. I would spend hours in the lane of our house singing Punjabi folk and Hindi film songs when Bauji was away on tours of the jails in Punjab and Papaji

---

* https://heritagetimes.in/royal-indian-navy-mutiny-1946

had left for work. Friends and even passers-by and vendors would stop to listen; my friends would say in appreciation, "Wah ji wah!" Of course, I sang songs and enacted film scenes only after Bauji and Papaji had left home for work. To take up the job as ticket collector was a choice I had made as I had no other dream but to go to Bambai and do some kind of work in films. On this job, I watched even the worst of films again and again. I enjoyed action films and songs the most. It was through these repeated watching sessions that I began to subconsciously learn that songs were intricately connected to the scenes of the film, the story and characters. Two decades later, the music composer S.D. Burman would say to me, "*Bakshi, film ka kahani theek se suno. Kahani main gaana hai* (Bakshi, listen to the film's story carefully. The songs are in the story)!" Many of my songs have the film's script condensed in their four verses . . . Within two years [of working at the cinema in Rawalpindi], my little world was destroyed forever. A storm arrived that uprooted not just me and my dreams, but millions from our ancestral land, *humari zameen, humari mitti.*'

* * *

The year was 1947. Pindi was predominately Hindu—they ran many of the businesses. In the villages surrounding Pindi, the Muslims were in a majority. Looting, burning of shops and homes, public hangings, abduction of women, it had all started before Partition. We heard rumours of similar violence happening across the border too. Many people on both sides of the border became 'outsiders' and refugees in their ancestral land before the actual date of Partition. Men were killed and women abducted. Most of the violence was planned and conducted by people not from Pindi; raiders arrived from nearby villages or from 'India' to grab what they could. Nand saw women being raped by rioters, and men and women being hanged from trees and lamp posts. He saw men's hands being hacked. He saw his relatives' and friends' homes and shops being burnt to scare their families to leave Punjab. This violence impacted him for life. Most people, on both sides of the border, who had managed to escape, could not carry anything beyond what they were wearing.

I once met the actor Dharmendra after Dad's passing, and he mentioned to me, 'Your daddy spoke often about his years in Pindi, and it reminded me of his song from *Jab Jab Phool Khile*, "Yahan Main Ajnabi Hoon". His nostalgia is symbolic in the verse, "... *mujhe yaad aa raha hai, woh chhota sa shikara.*"'

I have recounted the circumstances under which the Bakhshis had to flee their place of birth in the previous chapter. Nand's Bauji being the superintendent of police, Punjab Jails, could manage a safe passage for his family, unlike millions. The Dakota aircraft they flew on was occupied by their entire family and perhaps by some other refugees and police officers' families as well. These were the 'privileged'. The Bakhshis at least had each other, if not their home and valuables.

About what he had witnessed in the weeks leading up to Partition, Dad once confided in his dear friend P.N. Puri, who had known him as a friend right from his early days in Bombay in the 1960s. Dad had never spoken to us, his children, about this. This conversation, between Puri and Dad, took place in the same year Dad passed away. I began to meet with his friends and relatives, with film-makers, to document their moments with Dad. Puri told me, 'You know, beta, your daddy suffered from some phobias and anxieties related to being alone and abandoned. Some were because of the gruesome violence he had witnessed during the partition of India. He told me he had witnessed people being murdered, raped, burnt alive, and those images haunted him through his life. A family known to him in their village severed the head of the mother and cut the long hair of their teenage daughters to make them appear as boys—because worse things could happen when the "others" arrived. This anxiety was one of the reasons he always asked me, or one of his friends—like Dr Nanavati, or the car dealer Choksey, or Chhitar Mal, the friend from the railways—to accompany him during long-distance train journeys.'

Going back to the Bakhshis' journey across the turbulent border. They were transported safely to the air strip in a truck manned by the Gorkha Regiment, and then to Delhi. As Dad would say, '*Aur phir hum Dilli bas gaye* (And then we settled in Delhi).' He told me that they arrived in India on 2 October 1947. (He was to be married on this same date a few years later, in 1955, in Lucknow.) Within two weeks of their arrival, on 14 October 1947, the Bakhshis were registered as refugees at the office of the deputy superintendent police, Refugee Registration Branch, Poona. Anand Prakash realized he and his family had become 'refugees' only when he had to sign their names and mention their previous address in the refugee register.

The refugee certificate was granted to Anand Prakash one week before Diwali, on 3 November. For him, it must have been the only cause for cheer on the Diwali of that unfortunate year. But when he looked around, he felt they were so much better off than the others. They were all together in that moment of colossal loss, insecurity, financial ruin, uncertainty and fear. When we were children, he would often tell us, 'Look around, count your blessings.'

* * *

'*Duniya mein, kitna gham hai, mera gham kitna kam hai, duniya ka gham dekha toh, main apna gham bhool gaya*'

—*Amrit*

With their wealth and status gone and their dignity demolished overnight, the Bakhshis began a tattered new life.

They had chosen to receive, as refugees, cash compensation instead of land and moved from one sympathetic and helpful relative to another, from one rented premises to another, for the next few years, until they came to reside temporarily in Delhi's West Patel Nagar in 1954; in Netaji Nagar, Kalkaji, in 1961; in Kamla Nagar in 1971; and, eventually, in Basti Sarai Rohilla in 1972.

It eventually dawned on them that they would never go back to Pindi, as they were now regarded as unwanted outsiders in that city, with their house occupied by some strangers. Papaji and Biji had kissed the floor of the house before locking it and handing the keys to a trusted neighbour, telling them, 'We will be back soon when this madness is over.' Bauji had kissed the tarmac before taking off on the Dakota plane. Nand had carried with him the mitti (soil) of Pindi in a glass bottle emptied of its medicinal contents; it remained in his Godrej cupboard's steel vault throughout his life.

Biji now had to reassure her demoralized, scared and scarred family. She told them, '*Hindustan mein tumhein naye logon ki, naye rishton ki aur naye riwaazon ki aadat padh jayegi; ghabranein ki koi zaroorat nahi* (You will get used to the new people, new relations and new customs in India; no need to worry).'

In February 2002, a month before Dad passed away, he made plans with his dear friend Advocate Shyam Keswani, who had once been a refugee from Sindh, to visit Pindi after being discharged from the hospital. But it was not to be. The plan could not stand against the gradual weakening of his lungs from prolonged asthma. He passed away within a month's time. But his songs live on—cherished beyond our borders and in '*meri* Pindi, *mera pind* (my Rawalpindi, my village)' even today.

In his poem 'Rawalpindi', he expresses his anguish at having had to leave Pindi as a refugee. But for me, the poem resonates with anyone who has had to separate from something beautiful that had always belonged to them.

Pindi

Saaneha yeh meri zindagi seh gayi
Main yahan aa gaya woh wahan reh gayi.
Kuch na main kar saka dekhta reh gaya.
Kuch na woh kar saki dekhti reh gayi.

Log kehtey hain, taqseem sab ho gaya
Jo nahi batt saki cheez woh reh gayi.
Inn zameeno ne kitna lahoo pi liya
Yeh khabar aasmaano talak hai gayi.
Rastey pe khadi ho gayeen sarhadein
Sarhadon pe khadi bebasi reh gayi.
Yaad Pindi ki aati hai ab kisliye?
Meri mitti thi Jehlum mein woh beh gayi.
De gayi, ghar, gali, shehar mera kisey
Kya pataa kis se Bakhshi woh kya keh gayi.

* * *

Hausla

The loss of his Maaji at the age of six, leaving the gurukul in the middle of the term as a teenager, not making any headway in Lahore looking for work as a singer, the unceremonious dismissal from the navy, the loss of his pind at the age of seventeen—these tragedies, one after the other within a decade, marked just the beginning of the challenging phase of Nand's life. He would encounter and, luckily, survive each of the future challenges; he would tackle them all head-on! With just his hausla as his companion.

What Nand had with him as his rock-solid companions on this long and arduous journey—companions that no one could take away from him—were his *hausla*, *himmat*, *pratibha*, *zaroorat*, his discipline, his faith in his Bansi Wale (Lord Krishna), his poems, his ability to create his own compositions and sing them, and his family, us, who were to arrive later. To see better days, he knew he had to first accept and come to terms with his tragic present, which he did.

In their new land, the refugees, the Bakshis, needed work. His Bauji eventually got a job with the police in Ambala, Papaji got a job in a bank in Delhi. And to provide additional support to his displaced family, Nand enlisted in the Indian Army, the profession his Mohyal clan was proud of. He had done so in less than forty days after their arrival in India.

> *'Duniya mein rehana hai toh kaam kar pyare, khel koi naya subah-o-shaam kar pyare'*
>
> —*Haathi Mere Saathi*

3

1947–1950

'My Aim in Life'

'Watan pe jo fida hoga, amar woh naujawaan hoga'
                                        —*Phool Bane Angaare*

Anand Prakash joined the Indian Army, Corps of Signals, at the age of seventeen. On 15 November 1947, he was given the rank of signal man at the Signals Training Centre in Jubbulpore (now Jabalpur, in Madhya Pradesh).

The Corps of Signals provides military communication services to the army. They are the communications service providers to the formations, battalions, regiments and platoons, wherever they be located—in unit lines during a peace posting or on the move during a conflict zone posting. The Corps of Signals was formed in 1911, under Lieutenant Colonel S.H. Powell, and went on to make important contributions to World War I and World War II. Today, it possesses state-of-the-art modern techniques for meeting the communications requirements of the Indian Army in the twenty-first century.

Let us take a glimpse at an average fauji's regular day in a non-conflict zone, to quickly get an idea of what life in the army must have been like for the fauji Bakhshi.

Typically, a unit, i.e. a battalion or a regiment, stays together in a 'unit line', a complex that generally comprises barracks for the troops, playground, armoury, office buildings and a training centre. Every unit has a small school where classes are held regularly for the jawans and non-commissioned officers, to educate them and prepare them for various examinations.

The fauji's day begins much before sunrise. When the reveille (bugle or drum) is sounded, the jawans assemble in rank and file. Their platoon commander inspects them to check if they are neatly turned out. Then, they are moved 'on the double', marched off in a slow jog and later sent for vigorous exercises and running drills. An hour after breakfast, they assemble again for various training programmes and tasks (including weapons training, driving and classroom sessions, if applicable to the soldier). Then they proceed to the mess for lunch. The unit rests for an hour or two after lunch and assembles on the sports ground for some game or the other, like hockey, football or basketball, or they proceed to practise boxing or swimming.

Before sunset, the retreat bugle is sounded and the flag in the unit's quarter guard is lowered as the night guards arrive on duty. By sunset, the jawans are relatively free and may now wear mufti—a specified pattern of civilian clothes. They now get ready for a roll call, a physical count, after which the next day's schedule is announced. Then, they proceed to the unit line's recreation rooms for watching television or reading the newspaper. After dinner, at about 2200 hours, a bugle is sounded ordering 'lights out', and every jawan, except those on night guard, must go to bed. Every hour of a soldier's life is strictly regulated, with the bugle calls determining the pattern of their day.

As Dad would later recollect, 'Picturization of songs nowadays, with fifty dancers and the hero and heroine in the foreground, reminds me of my army days. We were fifty soldiers, led by our chief physical training officer in the foreground.'

Anand Prakash had only one motive to join the Indian Army: 'Depend on no one but yourself. Earn a livelihood to support your family.'

'Mushkil mein hai kaun kisika, samjho iss raaz ko, le kar apna naam kabhi tum khud ko, awaaz do'

—*Angaar*

* * *

Azad

In the signal corps, every operator of the unit's internal telephone exchange is provided with a code name so that their personal identity remains unknown if an enemy taps into their communications. 'AZAD' (free/freedom) was fauji Anand Prakash's code name. He remained in training and, later, in peace postings throughout his stint in the army. He still dreamt of going to Bombay and try his luck in films, but he'd put that dream on the back burner for the time being. Army life for a sipahi-level soldier is hard.

Yet Anand Prakash found a way to feed his artistic soul alongside the daily parades and drills:

'I would write my own nazms during breaks. In 1949, Raj Kapoor and Nargis's film *Barsaat* was released, and I watched it twenty times! I was fascinated by the songs, by Hasrat Jaipuri and Shankar Jaikishan, and the romance! I always had a romantic spirit. I would always return to the barracks and write down the songs of the film I had just watched. In a few months, I began writing the songs of *Barsaat* in my own words, as though I were the film's songwriter? I would do that only for the films I loved. Then I would sing these songs written by me to my comrades. They loved my creations, and I started becoming quite popular, soon even beyond my unit. The training was hard, and my writing and singing provided the entertainment that even my comrades looked forward to. When I would write patriotic or romantic nazms, it would elicit whistles and claps from my friends.

'Firing with my pen was my thing, not with guns, even though I felt immense pride in being a fauji. Our country had been born just two or three years ago, and everywhere we faujis travelled, even when we went back home on leaves, people around us made us feel very special.

'Writing poems and songs, and singing them to entertain my comrades, kept me going through all my years of vigorous training and being away from Biji and home. The Bara Khana events also came to my rescue. Talents from within the unit lines put up skits and musical dramas. I participated in every single one during both my stints in the army. Soon, even seniors across units got to know of me. I would be introduced as, "*Yeh hai woh fauji jo nazm likhta hai aur gaata bhi hai* (This is that soldier who writes and sings nazms)." Gradually, I began to feel very strongly that I should not be in the fauj for the rest of my life, that I would not grow here the way I wanted to.

'*Mere Bansi Wale ne mere kone kone mein sangeet ka prem bhar diya tha* (My Lord Krishna with his flute had filled every pore of my being with the love of music). The army was not the place to indulge those emotions. I wanted out, soon, but was clueless as to how to leave a secure job and travel to a new town without my family's support. They will never let me leave the army. The radio became my companion, and I would look forward to listening to the songs by writers like Madhok Sa'ab. He was my earliest influence as a lyricist. Mahakavi Dina Nath Madhok (1902–1982), along with Kidar Sharma and Pradeep are amongst the first generation of Hindi cinema's lyricists.'

* * *

Early Influences

Anand Bakshi began to truly appreciate lyrics in film songs when he listened to the songs of D.N. Madhok keenly. So Mahakavi Madhok became his first influence as a lyricist.

'Madhok Sa'ab set the standards for filmy *geet* writing back in the 1950s. We lyricists of today are following in his great footsteps; well,

I am at least. *Main* D.N. Madhok Sa'ab *ka fan tha* (I was his fan). He was a man of the masses. He taught me that the first aim of the lyricist is to get through to people, and for that purpose simple words are the most effective. Simple words help make simple music, which gets across easily. Madhok Sa'ab's songs taught me that the first and most important thing is to get to people in the very first hearing. Madhok Sa'ab *ka rang hi kuch aur tha* (had a different colour). His simplicity in lyrics writing inspired my own lyrics-writing style. He advised me, "Bakshi, choose simple words. Don't ever forget that your songs have to be heard and understood all over the nation by a variety of people." If people appreciate the simplicity of my lyrics, it is not only because I am not educated beyond eighth standard and have a very limited Hindi vocabulary, as I was educated in Urdu, but also because his advice to use simple language kept me in check. From him I learnt to use rhyming words in the same verse. For example, in "*Chupp gaye saare nazaare, oye kya baat ho gai*", I rhymed many meaningful words in the same verse, "*Chodh meri 'baiyyan', padhun tere 'paiyyan', taaron ki 'chaiyyan' mein 'saiyyan'*." I also learnt from Madhok Sa'ab that I should suggest Punjabi folk tunes to my music composers along with my lyrics because I sometimes wrote using Punjabi music metres.'

The other important influences on Anand Bakshi were Sahir Ludhianvi and Shailendra.

'Sahir Ludhianvi introduced me to some producers and encouraged me to write. So did Shailendra. I admire Sahir Sa'ab personally for his noble heart, and professionally for blending *shayari* into a film-song situation. I learnt from him how to weave simple words into shayari. Once, when I was looking for work and was demoralized and clueless as to how to proceed, I had asked Sahir Sa'ab how to make inroads into the film industry, how to find work. And Sahir told me, "Bakshi, either you call on people, or people call you. There is no other way to get work in this business!" So on his advice I made it a point to meet five to six film people daily to ask them for work. And after nearly two to three years of meeting at least five to six film people every day—including actors, producers, directors, music composers, even their assistants and managers, sound recordists, musicians—I did find some producers and directors who gave me a hearing, and gradually, I began to get one or two songs to write for their films. But I admire Sahir Sa'ab most for his blending of *shayari* into film-song situations. I learnt how to weave shayari, poetry, into filmy geet from him.

'Shailendra and his simple folk songs are simply marvellous. They tug at your heart at the very first hearing! *Kya baat hai unki* (What can one say of them)! Folk songs are simple and not always poetic, but they have a lot of depth—I learnt that from Shailendra's lyrics-writing style. He even recommended me to producers, such a secure and noble soul he was. I think even Shailendra's lyrics have contributed to literature and not of just those lyricists who claimed to be "poets".

'So these three are my gurus too, apart from Bismil Saeedi Sa'ab. I thank them for where I find myself today. The lyricist Ram Prakash Ashq also encouraged me a lot to find work. I thank all these poets and writers for the success of many of my songs. I am still nowhere near the greats like Hasrat, Sahir, Neeraj, Majrooh, Jan Nisar, Narendra Sharma, Shailendra, and some others. I liked hearing Kaifi Azmi's songs too.

'Some people have criticized me for doing just *tukbandi*, rhyming. But I have never claimed to be a poet. I am essentially a song specialist, a film songwriter, and not really a poet, even though some people consider me one. Sahir Sa'ab was a true poet. I am just a songwriter, and I even admitted it in *Bobby*—"Main Shayar Toh Nahin"— and then again in Shaktida's *Ajnabi*—"*Janeman, jan-e-jigar, hota mein shayar agar, likhta ghazal teri adaon par.*"

'When I arrived in Bombay, I had just begun writing songs for films. But before I got noticed by the industry, it was Madhok Sa'ab, and later even Shailendra, who graciously advised me to use *sadharan lafz* (ordinary words), *saral* Hindustani in my lyrics, and not much Urdu, so that my songs could be heard and appreciated across the country.

'Until then, I had been using a lot of Urdu words in my songs. Perhaps because I was educated in the Urdu script, and I was maybe subconsciously trying to compete with those who ruled the roost in the '50s—some lyricists who were also renowned poets and used a lot of Urdu. So I used a lot of Urdu in my early writings, from the early '60s. But with the success of *Jab Jab Phool Khile* (1965) and *Farz* (1967) in particular, I realized the true value of writing within the limitations of my Hindi vocabulary. What I had believed was my shortcoming was to become my so-called 'genius' years later. Even when I wrote nazms and plays for the army's Bara Khanas, I used a lot of Urdu. A lot of my peers were educated in Punjab and had studied in the Urdu medium and appreciated my Urdu poems, so I hadn't realized that I should use saral Hindustani while writing filmy geet.

'When the songs of *Farz*, which I had written using conversational Hindustani, became superhits, I began to use conversational Hindi in many more songs. But at the same time, I always kept the characters of the story in mind, so that the listener does not feel that the words the character is singing don't belong to him or her and rather belong to me, the lyricist. If I am visible in a song, I have failed as a film song lyricist, even if I succeed as a poet. I wrote "simple" effortlessly as I had a limited Hindi vocabulary. When I arrived here in the '50s, I did not know that what I considered my weakness—not being an Urdu mushaira shayar— was actually to become my strength. It made my songs the songs of the common man. Some journalists began to call me the poet of the masses.

* * *

'Army life and nazm writing went on. Soon, on 18 June 1949, I graduated as "Switch Board Operator", Class III, from the Signals Training Centre in Jubbulpore.'

Maturing to being a young adult by 1949 and encouraged by his comrades and seniors to leave the army, Nand began to concentrate on writing songs and became the person he really was underneath the fauji uniform. He wrote to Papaji, hinting he may leave the army and go to Bombay to join the film industry. He mentioned that he felt like he did not belong in the army. Bauji wrote to him several letters, warning him not to leave. In a correspondence dated 21 December 1949, Papaji warned his Azeez not to leave the Hindustani fauj—this job of honour and security—for a career in 'kanjar *waale kaam*' (the work of kanjars). He told Nand that it would be foolish of him to go to an alien land where they knew no one, that if he did so he was destined to fail in this fruitless dream of joining a worthless profession, wiping out his precious savings in the process. They had yet to recover from the losses imposed on them by Partition. And if he failed, the army would not take him back.

'Naturally, they were a worried and upset lot. As a father, I would have been upset too. It was just three years since we became homeless and here I was leaving a secure *sarkari naukri* (government job)! I respected them for their views, but I had a dream to follow and had to work extra hard to prove them all wrong one day!'

From that same period, there is a letter from his maternal uncle W.M. Major Bali, posted in Jodhpur then, telling his nephew *not* to leave the army or else he would repent later, telling him not to act in haste. But, his uncle added, if he was hell-bent on leaving then he had to first pass first class in English. It was the language of the gentry in cities, and it would impress people in Bombay, making it easier for an ex-fauji like him to find a well-paying, decent job if he failed to secure work in films.

'Their anger and their harsh words for my dream not only hurt me but also made me very angry. I knew I could write well, but they turned a complete deaf ear to me because of the family's honour and their ancestral conditioning that the fauj was a "secure" job for the now middle-class refugees like us. Two years ago, we were among the wealthy families in Pindi. I would fill all the pockets of my clothes daily with an assortment of expensive dry fruits to gorge on and share with many friends freely. The trauma of Partition, the fact that we'd lost our wealth and dignity overnight, had made them cowards, I felt. However, I strongly believed that living in the fauj, with just basic food and basic comforts, had made me very capable of being able to survive in Bambai. *Main saharon pe nahi, khud pe yakin rahkta hoon. Gir padoonga toh hua kya, main sambhal jaoonga* (I don't count on support and always believe in myself. So what if I stumble? I will regain balance myself). I decided to pen down my ambitions, sign the note and put it up on the wall, so that I can see it every day and not forget my dream and my path ahead. It was henceforth to become my primary *aim in life*.'

Nand's half-sister, Shubi Khem Datt, recalls, 'In our Delhi family home, when Nand was on a leave and visiting us, he had written one word on the wall: Bambai.'

* * *

'My Aim in Life'

On 24 January 1950, while he was in the army, Anand Prakash Bakhshi wrote his first personal manifesto, which he called 'Aim in Life':

Everyone in this world, rich or poor, should have a definite aim in life. A man without any fixed purpose in life is like a ship without a rudder, at the mercy of the winds, powerless to control its course. So, a person having no aim in life has nothing by which to guide his actions or regulate his conduct. I, the undersigned, Anand Prakash Bakshi (AZAD), intend to study music. For it is my aim in life to become an artist. And to achieve this, I must join films, radio or theatre, and become a singer, song composer, music director, director, etc.

More than three decades later, on 10 October 1988, he added a footnote to his 'Aim in Life':

So it happened: I became a successful songwriter. Earned name, fame, money, flats, cars and whatnot. But somehow on this road of life I lost my self-confidence. I became Anand Bakshi from Anand Prakash. Now I want to again become Anand Prakash from Anand Bakshi. I think I have done it once, so I will do it again. God help me. In these thirty-eight years, I have made mistakes. I wish to be excused for these. I didn't know what I was doing.

Let us look closely at this footnote. It perhaps reflects his fear of being abandoned and left alone that began to overwhelm him from the '70s. His Mamaji, Major Bali, believed that Nand had suffered a trauma because of the loss of his Maaji and because he began living away from home at an early age. His friend P.N. Puri believed that Nand had been traumatized by Partition, which he had witnessed at the young age of seventeen. We will never know the exact truth.

In the mid-'90s, to cure himself of this fear of loneliness or abandonment, he began to travel alone by local trains in Mumbai every week. This was his attempt at reliving his life once again as Anand Prakash, the fauji. For this purpose, he first took a local train on 9 March 1995, after a gap of nearly thirty years. He rode from the Khar station to Bandra, reciting his own lyrics to himself:

'Gaadi bula rahi hai, seeti baja rahi hai, chalna hi zindagi hai, chalti hi ja rahi hai'

—Dost

* * *

Birth of the Poet

Back in Nand's army days, his Bauji and Papaji had assumed that their Azeez had found his bearings in army life. What they did not know was that their fauji beta had been regularly writing poems and plays and had given himself a pen-name: Anand Prakash Bakhshi. Interestingly, at every stage of his life, he referred to himself differently: his parents named him Anand; but his parents, family and even he addressed himself as Nand; Nando (by his distant relatives); Anand Prakash, the school student and naval cadet; Bakhshi Anand Prakash Vaid, the fauji; Anand Prakash Bakhshi, the poet; and eventually, geetkaar Anand Bakshi, when he became a lyricist. (A film producer had misspelt his surname, dropping the 'h'! The name, of course, stuck for good. However, in his legal documents and signatures on photographs he handed out to fans, he always wrote the name Bakhshi, with an 'h'.)

The Indian Army's Corps of Signals unit was where he nurtured his writing skills and talent. The encouragement he received from his peers and seniors inspired and emboldened him in his dream of leaving the army and trying his luck in Bombay. While he was in the fauj, he spent a significant amount of time in the Jubbulpore and Hyderabad divisions. Always looking up to his seniors and keen to earn their respect—soldiers are built like that—Anand Prakash Bakhshi was greatly motivated when General Dubey, an officer who was popular and well respected in the ranks, encouraged him to leave the army for a career in films as a writer. But Bakhshi felt he also needed someone who was an established poet to offer him feedback and criticism on his writing. Even though he considered D.N. Madhok and Shailendra to be his gurus, they were out of reach for him to get their feedback.

He began to seek a professional mentor who could guide him with his writing and teach him formally how poetry was written by the masters. And he was soon to meet an editor and poet, respected in the literary circles of Purani Dilli and other places across India where his publication travelled. His name was Bismil Saeedi. Bakhshi had known Saeedi; he was a regular reader of *Beeswi Sadi*, an Urdu monthly edited by Saeedi. Bakhshi and Saeedi were to become close friends one day, and their friendship began when Saeedi Sa'ab became a mentor to the young amateur poet and fauji. If you are a fan of

Anand Bakshi, let me share with you the contribution Saeedi Sa'ab made to the shaping of his imagination.

'Bismil Saeedi Sa'ab was the first person who suggested and encouraged me to read more poetry books written by the legends of Urdu and Farsi poetry. He corresponded regularly with me while I was in the army, and I would visit him in Purani Dilli whenever I was on leave. He was generous with his time and criticism, and would continue to be so over the next decade and more. He held and guided my pen after I began writing poetry intensely and in earnest, 1950 onwards.'

I will elaborate more on their special relationship in Chapter 5, about Bakhshi's second stint in the army, from 1951 to 1956. This was when their acquaintanceship blossomed into friendship and gave the fauji that so far elusive extra confidence to surrender his uniform and gun for what was to become a lasting relationship with his pen.

The budding poet was determined to leave the fauj, but he was a great believer in luck and was waiting for a manifestation of good luck. Within two months of his penning his 'Aim in Life' note, an event occurred that became his desired sign of good luck. It broke the formidable dam that was holding him back from leaving the army.

* * *

Manifestation of luck: *'Luck bhi zaroori hai'*

Fauji Anand Prakash Bakhshi's second poem was published on 25 March 1950 in the army's prestigious magazine *Sainik Samachar*. (The first was published when he was living in Rawalpindi.) He had requested the editor of *Sainik Samachar* to mention his rank along with his name so that he could impress his comrades and seniors.

The poem reflects the pathos and suffering of someone praying for a break from the deluge of bad luck and prolonged unfortunate circumstances. The poet is challenging God, nature and circumstance.

He is asking a question: 'How can my talent and prayers be denied?' The day will come when all the forces ranged against him will accept him, and help him fulfil his dream and ambition.

> *Girengi bijliyan kab tak, jalenge aashiyaan kab tak,*
> *Khilaf ehle-chaman ke tu rahega aasman kab tak?*
> *Satayega, rulayega, jaleyega jahaa kab tak,*
> *Zameer, zeheno, jism, jaan se, niklega dhuan kab tak?*
> *Nizam-e-gulistaan, ehle-gulistan hi sambhalenge,*
> *Teri manmaniyan, teri hukumatt, baaghban kab tak?*
> *Hamari badnaseebi ki aakhir koi hadh hogi,*
> *Rahoge hum par tum, na meherban, eh meherbaan, kab tak?*
> *Meri aankhen barasti hein musalsal hijr mein Bakhshi,*
> *Mukabil inke barsengi bhala ye badliyan kab tak?*

Two decades later, in 1976, *Sainik Samachar* featured geetkaar Anand Bakshi. In this feature, Bakshi mentioned that the publication of his 1950 poem was 'a manifestation of good luck', inspiring him to 'try my luck in films'.

* * *

'Logon ka kaam hai kehna'

On 10 April 1950, less than three months after having written his Aim in Life statement and within a month of the *Sainik Samachar* poem, fauji Anand Prakash requested a discharge from the fauj, turning a deaf ear to the opinions of his family elders.

It was the boldest step Nand had ever taken against the wishes of his family. This was to be the first in a series of even more desperate and drastic steps he would take in life, as he believed in tadbeer (our actions that shape our destiny) rather than in taqdeer (our preordained destiny).

4

1950–1951

'Yahan Main Ajnabi Hoon'

'Kaise koi, jaane bhala, khwabon ki taabeer, aakash pe, baitha huwa,
likhta hai taqdeer; kis rang se, jaane bane, jeevan ki tasveer, aakash pe,
baitha huwa, likhta hai taqdeer'

—Taqdeer

Anand Prakash Bakhshi had been in Bombay once before, for a day
or perhaps two, in October 1947, when the Bakhshi family had to
register for their refugee certificates in Poona, at the office of the
superintendent of police, Naigaum.

'Mujhe gaane ka shauk bachpan se tha, lekin main geetkar banne ka
sapna liye Bambai aaya (I had dreamt about becoming a singer since
childhood, but it was with the dream of becoming a lyricist that I
came to Bombay). In 1950, I arrived at the Dadar station with all my
savings, of Rs 300–400, and a handful of poems, some of which got
recorded as film songs many years later. Meri himmat, mera hausla, meri
pratibha aur meri zaroorat mere saath thee (My courage, my confidence,
my talent and my need were with me). I was also confident that my
two years of training in the navy and three in the army had made be
capable of surviving anywhere. On my first day here, at the Dadar
station, I was overwhelmed by the crowd. I had never seen so many

people. . . No one in this city made eye contact . . . I knew no one here! I felt alone. I felt I could not do this alone and would ask my Bansi Wale for help. I wrote a prayer before I stepped out of the station, to give myself hausla aur himmat.'

> *Mere Bhagwan, Bansi Wale,*
> *Tu ne mujhe jazbaat diye,*
> *Sangeet ka prem mere jism ke kone kone mein bhar diya,*
> *Main tera ehsaan mand hoon.*
> *Aur ab main tere saamne jhuk kar, apne unn haseen khwabon ki*
>   *taabeer mangta hoon,*
> *Jo tune meri masoom ankhon mein basaye.*

Tera Nand

More than twenty years later, on 12 February 1971, geetkar Anand Bakshi wrote his second prayer. He thanked Lord Krishna for helping him achieve his aim in life. He had signed his first prayer as Nand, and he signed his second one as Anand Prakash Bakhshi, not as 'Anand Bakshi', the name he had acquired in the film world after 1956. Whenever he wanted to connect to his roots, he would address himself as Nand, and when he wanted to connect with his fauji spirit and needed help from God he addressed himself as Anand Prakash Bakhshi. Anand Bakshi never conformed to the idea of 'Anand Bakshi'.

> *BHAGWAN Bansi wale, main tera bachcha hoon. Yeh shayad meri doosri prayer hai. Mujhe apne aim in life main kaamyabi mili. Yeh teri hi kripa se hua. Warna main iss kaabil kahan tha ke main itna mashoor aadmi bann jaoon. Hazaaron laakhon rupay kamaoon.*
>   *Aaj main tere saamne jhukh ke ek prarthana karta hoon. Mere dil se yeh darr aur wahem nikaal de. Mujhe hausla, himmat de. Maine*

apne paon mein jo aap hi jo darr ke beri daali hai jald kaat ke phenk
de. Mujhe azaad kar de.
     Mujhe mere biwi bachchon ke saath sach se jeene de.
     Mera Khoya huwa wiswas waapas de.
     12 February 1971. Anand Bakhshi.

Having arrived in Bombay, he hung around at the waiting room for passengers at the Dadar railway station for a while and then stepped out. He checked into a dormitory nearby, in Dadar West, meant for migrants.

     'Earlier, I had always been surrounded either by my comrades in the army or family back home. Bombay was a place I had seen only in films and read about in magazines, and I felt it would welcome my talent with open arms, as my peers in the army had done; they made me feel like a war hero, the way they loved my writing and singing. But when I arrived in Bombay looking for work, I was an unseen drop in the ocean. No one even acknowledged my presence. It was even impossible for me to get an entry into the company of the ruling songwriters who were great poets too. *Geetkar banne ka masoom sapna liye main Bambai ki sadhkon pe ghoomta tha,* film studios *dhoondta tha, aankhon mein masoom sapna aur dil mein chhota sa hausla liye* (My innocent dream of becoming a lyricist made me roam the streets of Bombay, where I looked for film studios, with this innocent dream in my eyes and a little bit of courage in my heart).

     'Soon, I began to feel like a stranger in Bombay. To make matters worse, the relative I was counting on to put me up for at least a week or two, till I found work, did not agree to do so, for whatever reason. I began to miss my army life and home. I felt like my song from *Jab Jab Phool Khile*, "*Kabhi pehele dekha nahin yeh sama, ke main bhool se aa gaya hoon kahan. Yahan main, ajnabi hoon.*"'

     Anand Bakhshi expresses this sentiment, of a stranger in a strange land who misses the familiar warmth of home, in another song, from the film *Dard Ka Rishta*: 'Iss shehar se accha tha, bahot apna wo gaon, panghat hai yahan koi na peepal ki wo chaaon.'

'I had a close relative living in Bombay, and I was counting on her giving me shelter in her house for a few days, until I found my bearings in the new city and a guest house close to the area where I had to go looking for work in films. Her family were close relatives of my Papaji and Bauji. When I reached her house, she welcomed me, but when she realized I was expecting her to host me for a few days, her attitude towards me changed dramatically. When I ate a small meal and washed my face and hands, she accused me of dirtying her washbasin and said that I needed to learn to be more upper class. She had no clue how dignified and disciplined army jawans are. But I soon realized she was acting cruel suddenly because she did not know how to turn me away. I told her I had already found accommodation with an army mate and left her home. Strangely, after two decades, she became a family friend, but I never reminded her how she had treated me when, for her, I was just a "zero".

'I found out that there was a famous studio in Dadar itself. I checked into a guest house in Dadar after my relative had refused to let me stay with her even for one night, and I hunted down the nearest film studio soon. The gateman would not let me enter. I waited for the duty hour to change and hired a taxi just to enter. While I waited outside for a few days trying to get in, I realized that the gatemen would unquestioningly allow taxis to enter. I entered the complex in a taxi, and it was my good luck that I met the owner of Kardar Studio— actor, producer and director Abdul Rashid Kardar! I was dressed very neatly, thanks to my army years, and I confidently walked up to him, uninterrupted by anyone, and told him, "*Main shayar hoon. Dilli se aaya hoon. Geet likhna chahta hoon* (I am a shayar, from Delhi, and I want to write lyrics)." This was my very first meeting with a film personality. I thought this was quite easy, now I knew how to approach and enter these fortresses of the film world. Mr Kardar's mood changed a bit when he realized that I was just a "struggler" looking for work. But he kindly put me on to one of his managers or assistants and walked away.

'His manager heard my poems and told me he would report to Mr Kardar. I tried to meet film-makers, music composers, by taking tips from the gatemen at studios. Some were kind and shared with me the addresses, while some shooed me away. But I could not meet a single film-related personality thereafter. I lost hope within three months of my arrival when I ran out of money. Discreetly and hiding from ticket checkers, I began to stay at the waiting room for passengers at the Dadar station, to save on room rent.

'I could not make any headway even on the theatre front. No one I knew gave me any leads on how to meet the theatre wallahs. However, my aim in life came to my rescue. It was etched in my mind, and I knew that one opportunity to remain connected to films still awaited me, even if I had to leave Bambai and return to my hometown Delhi. So I decided to take a shot at being a radio announcer. Things were not that bad for me as yet, I thought, and booked my ticket to Dilli. I thought radio would keep me connected to my aim in life, and once I got the job and settled down in radio, I would make another attempt at returning to Bambai.'

Anand Prakash Bakhshi made his way back to Dilli in December 1950. I was told by his Bhua (stepsister) that he wrote the song 'Gaadi Bula Rahi Hai' during a train journey. It's likely that he wrote this song back then. If you look closely at the inspiring verses, you may agree with my belief.

Nand knew that his family was angry and upset at his leaving the army, but General Dubey had told him that an ex-soldier can return if he had been discharged on his personal request before the completion of his terms of enrolment. However, Nand was confident that he would get the radio job, because he had been singing songs since childhood for one and all.

Once in Delhi, he lied to and reassured the family elders that he would be re-enlisting in the Corps of Signals. He told them that this was possible as he had taken voluntary discharge and, unlike his unfortunate exit from the navy, had not been dismissed from the army. So without informing anyone, the ever-optimistic Anand Prakash Bakhshi discreetly applied for the mandatory voice test at the All India Radio (AIR). His maternal uncle Major Bali helped him get an appointment for this test.

On 22 December 1950, Anand Prakash Bakhshi reported for the voice test at the AIR offices near India Gate. And he failed the test. He was shocked beyond belief as people had loved his singing since his childhood, and he had been a favourite at the army Bara Khanas too.

'For the first time since leaving the army, I began to contemplate returning to the army. I booked my train ticket to Jubbulpore.'

> 'Main shayar badnaam, main chala, main chala, mehfil se naakaam, main chala, main chala,
> Mere ghar se tumko, kuchh saaman milega, deewane shayar ka, ek diwan milega,
> Aur ek cheeze milegi, toota khali jaam, main chala, main chala, main shayar badnam'

—Namak Haraam

5

1951–1956

A Daughter Gives Birth to a
Father and Lyricist

Anand Prakash Bakhshi returned to the army soon on 16 February 1951, at the Jubbulpore division in Madhya Pradesh. He enrolled in the Corps of Signals for the second time and was sent to the EME division (the corps of electrical and mechanical engineers). Over the next two years, he trained here and qualified as 'electrician, Class III' on 11 September 1953.

* * *

'I could not bear the loud sounds of the infantry guns'

After qualifying as an automobile electrician, Bakhshi was posted to the infantry division at a salary of Rs 75 a month. One of the postings he was sent to was Jammu and Kashmir. The first thing that struck the fauji in the infantry division was the sound of big guns. He hated them! I recollect now that when he was at home working—he wrote most of his songs in his bedroom or in our living room—any unusual loud sound would disturb him immensely. He would leave his writing immediately and look for the source of the sound. Sound of the doorbell, the cooker whistling in the kitchen, us siblings shouting or singing loud, he was nearly oblivious to all that.

He was very sensitive to noise. In the mid-'70s, we had shifted to a brand-new five-bedroom house in Bandra West, and within three months we had to move out because the soft tinkle of the BEST public transport bus would 'disturb' him. This residential building was situated beside the main road; so we shifted to a quaint street off the main road nearby that had no heavy vehicles plying.

'In the army, we had to march left-right-left-right all day long. I even began to dream of marching! The loud sounds of heavy artillery guns in the infantry division disturbed me; they reminded me of the violence I had seen during Partition as a seventeen-year-old boy. I began to feel even more strongly than before that this was not my cup of tea. Most importantly, I felt I would lose touch with my need to be an artist and my passion for writing if I continued being a soldier. No one was interested to meet me the last time I was in Bombay. I thought if I could get a letter of recommendation from an army senior, I would be able to convince film people in Bombay that I had the talent and that they should hear my poems. So I decided to seek a recommendation letter from someone senior who truly believed I should leave the army the second time for my passion and talent for writing songs. Captain Varma *ki jai ho* (Long live Captain Varma)!'

I am reminded of something that happened during his second stint with the army. Bakhshi had to travel to Hyderabad for a personal visit to meet a relative. He embarked on the train while it was in the railway yard so he could get an unreserved seat. But before he could get inside the compartment, the train began to move. He stood on the steps leading up to the compartment and could not get in as the door was locked.

Holding the compartment railing in one hand and his tin suitcase in the other, he was horrified when he realized that the platform was higher than the steps he was standing on. The fast-approaching platform was only a few meters away when he began to shout and scream at the people inside who had locked the door so that no one else could enter until the train stopped at the platform. He was wearing army fatigues. Someone took pity on his screams for help, opened the door and gave him a hand. Just when he stepped into the compartment, the train reached the platform. He realized that had the door had remained unlocked for another few seconds, he would have lost both his legs. He told us later that this was among the most traumatic moments of his life. We still have the tin suitcase and have placed it in our living room, to remind us of his army origins.

* * *

The Unsung Hero

When Anand Prakash Bakhshi returned to the army for the second time, he made an extra effort to stay in touch with his poet and editor acquaintance Bismil Saeedi, to nurture their acquaintanceship into a friendship and to learn from him as a mentor. He felt he needed to improve his writing before he made another attempt for Bambai.

Saeedi's guidance stood the fauji and amateur poet in good stead and helped him evolve as a poet through the '50s and '60s. He believed that Saeedi was not just his '*meherbaan dost*' (generous friend) but also one of the two unsung heroes of his success story. (The second was Chhitar Mal Swaroop, a ticket collector for Western Railway. I will introduce you to this *farishta* I consider Nand's second mother in the next chapter. In a way, it was Chhitar Mal's good deed that gifted us the geetkar the film profession came to know.)

* * *

'*Mere meherbaan dost, Bismil Saeedi*'

Bismil Saeedi Sa'ab hailed from Tonk, Rajasthan, and lived near Jama Masjid in Delhi. He was an editor and Urdu poet who mainly wrote ghazals. Ages ago, he had been a disciple of the great poet Nazeer Akbarabadi. For a long time, Saeedi was associated with the Urdu monthly *Beeswien Sadi* (Twentieth Century), published from Purani Dilli. Dad was a regular reader of this magazine until his last years. I sometimes accompanied Dad to his favourite news stalls in Khar and Bandra, where he went every month just to buy the current issue of *Beeswien Sadi*. He would get totally engrossed in reading this magazine. When he travelled to Delhi on leave, he made it a point to meet Saeedi Sa'ab and seek feedback on his freshly penned nazms.

In 1998, on Anand Bakshi's sixty-eighth birthday party, hosted by Subhash Ghai, lyricist Javed Akhtar called Anand Bakshi the Nazeer Akbarabadi of our time. Nazeer Akbarabadi was an eighteenth-century Indian poet known as the 'father of nazm'; he wrote ghazals and nazms in Urdu under the nom de plume 'Nazeer'. At that time, it wasn't known to people that the poet Anand Prakash Bakshi was a disciple of, Bismil Saeedi, was himself a disciple of Akbarabadi. So Javed Akhtar had got that link right.

In their correspondence Saeedi addressed Bakhshi affectionately as 'Azeezi-o-Muhibbi', and Bakhshi would sign off as 'Tumhara Taalim' (*taalim* means student). I consider Saeedi Sa'ab as one of the primary pillars who provided crucial support to the amateur poet's life. Bakhshi would soon welcome another towering and supportive personality in his life, whom he went on to term as 'the pillar of my life with whose support I stand tall': Kamla.

* * *

'Ladki cycle wali, oye ladki cycle wali'

Subedar Amar Singh Mohan and family had arrived as refugees from Rawalpindi in 1947. Back in Pindi, they lived on the same street as the

Bakhshis and were acquaintances as they belonged to the same Mohyal clan. Post-Partition, Amar Singh Mohan and his family travelled to Ambala, then to Nagpur and eventually settled in Lucknow. Amar Singh served in the army as a subedar in Nagpur, and his family was settled in in Alambagh, Lucknow. This was to become the home of Anand Prakash Bakhshi's future in-laws.

Bakhshi's *bua* (his father's sister), Shanta Bua, was married in the extended family of Amar Singh. Shanta Bua once visited Amar Singh's home and on being introduced to his youngest daughter, Kamla, found her to be a good match for her fauji nephew, Bakhshi. Shanta Bua revealed her intention via a postcard she sent home on 2 September 1954, 'I have seen a Mohyal girl for Nand to marry. Her name is Kamla. She is the daughter of a retired army subedar living in Lucknow. He runs a cycle shop along with my daughter-in-law's father. Kamla is his youngest and only unmarried daughter among the three sisters. Kamla is fair-skinned, good-looking, a little plump, knows sewing and tailoring, and rides a cycle.'

The match was made quickly, and within a few days the weeding was announced. It was to take place in less than a month's time, as the fauji Bakhshi had a limited number of annual leaves. At his wedding in Lucknow, Anand Bakhshi met his good friend and neighbour Bhagwant Mohan from Pindi. Excited to meet a 'Pindiwala', he asked Bhagwant what he was doing at this wedding. Bhagwant replied, 'I am here for my sister Kamla's wedding. What are you doing here?' Bakhshi replied, 'It seems I'm marrying your sister!'

Bhagwant Mama (uncle) later told me, 'As a teenager, your daddy would sing film song parodies and his own written and tuned songs seated outside his house and entertain friends or anyone willing to stop and listen. My father and mother were livid that their *jawai* (son-in-law) left the fauj for films, but I was not surprised.'

* * *

Dilwale Dulhania Le Jayenge

Anand Prakash Bakhshi and Kamla Mohan got married in Lucknow on 2 October 1954. Exactly eight years before, on this same date, he and his family had escaped from 'Pakistan' as refugees.

In the early years of their marriage, Bakhshi's wife (our mother) would not keep well, so the fauji had to take leaves and travel to Delhi to look after her at his Papaji's house. Since he was in a peace posting, he was allowed the leaves. During the day, he would fulfil his army responsibilities, or, if he was at home, serve his father and wife; and at night he would entertain friends with his singing and writing.

Many years later, in 1967, geetkar Anand Bakshi received an inland letter from Major Gurmeet S. Sekhon (6th Mahar Regiment, Borders), who was his batch mate in the EME. Major Gurmeet said that he decided to write the letter when he heard Bakhshi's interview on the radio and saw his photograph in *Star & Style* magazine.

He wrote, 'Anand, I remember you as the fauji who lived with me in my camp, and we were both fond of singing. We would make each other hear the songs we sang. You would move your head a lot while singing. You would always tell me excitedly, "Gurmeet Paaji, tonight I'm going to make you hear something new I have written." You liked to write too. We performed in drama together, and you would tell me that I should play female roles until my face matured. I must tell you, after you left, I did not perform until I had grown a beard and looked manly enough. You would write songs in my notebook during our EME days. I don't have your address, so I have sent this letter to you addressed to *Filmfare* magazine. I hope it reaches you.'

Bakhshi's poetry 'tuitions' with Bismil Saeedi were going well. So, he began to plan his second attempt at trying his luck in Bombay. However, he believed that he still lacked the luck. He had failed once and could not afford another failure. So he needed more than just his belief in his talent to leave the army the second time. He was married now, and his wife was expecting a baby in a few months. An ardent believer in luck and God, as well as in taqdeer and tadbeer, Bakhshi looked forward to a sign from above before taking the plunge once again.

Anand and Kamla Bakhshi's firstborn, Suman (Pappi), arrived on 14 May 1956. Bakhshi remembered what his Biji had once said, '*Betiyan, piyoh de liye achcha naseeb laandi hain* (Daughters bring good luck for their fathers).' Suman's birth was the good-luck sign, the miracle he had been praying for!

Dad would later tell us, 'Your dream is a chance. If you take it, it's risky. If you do not take it, it's dangerous. Moreover, the army taught me that you cannot cross a bridge before it comes. But you must keep in sight the ones you will need to cross one day. And there is no bridge that cannot be crossed.'

His daughter's birth became the bridge he needed, to cross the chasm between the fauji he was and the geetkar he always wanted to be. As Bakhshi always believed, courage is taking a step forward into an area of difficulty, without a solution in mind, trusting that somehow help will become available. And so, Bakhshi put in his papers for the second time, mentioning 'discharge at my own request' in his resignation letter. 'Bambai, *wapas aa raha hoon main* (Bombay, I am coming back)!' With his limited savings in hand, and without the permission of his family, wife and in-laws, he took off his uniform, this time for good.

I once asked Dad who his favourite was among us four siblings. He replied, 'Pappi (Suman). She is the only one among you four who experienced my worst days financially and my years of anger and frustration before I made it. You three were born in my better days. She is the only one who took the brunt of my initial suffering.'

Before we move on to the next chapter of his life, to his formative years in films, let me share some of his thoughts on what army life gave him.

'The army, and even the Indian Railways because I travelled across the nation during my army years only on trains, taught me the value of time and commitment—ideals that I put into practice when delivering songs on time to producers and directors. Respect for seniors, respect for order. I treated the needs of my producers, because they were paying me to do a job, like a senior officer's orders.* The Army and railways taught me punctuality. I don't think a single song recording got delayed or cancelled because of me.† My producers and directors respect me the most for my discipline, over and above the box-office success of our films. The army taught me secularism. I lived happily among soldiers of various religions, despite the fact that in 1947 I had become a refugee overnight because of "hatred and politics". Like in the army, we film-makers laugh, cry, sing together. We are a fantastic example of national integration. The only drawback is that here, success is claimed by everybody, and nobody is willing to take the blame for a film's failure. Even after I left the army, I helped them get actors, star singers and composers for their entertainment programmes, as they need some relaxation after working in stressful conditions, risking their lives. My army commanding officer (Infantry Division) would tell us that in the army there are no runners-up, just winners. Be a winner, a prisoner, or be dead. I strived to be a winner, number one. I applied all these learnings to my writing profession. Every song for me was like the daily army drill.'

Having taken the decision to leave the army for the second time, Anand Bakhshi asked his guru Bismil Saeedi for guidance and his blessings. On 12 July 1956, Saeedi wrote a most encouraging letter to Bakhshi:

Azeezi Va Maha-Habibi Anand Prakash Sahab Bakhshi!
    Qudrat ne apko shaayarana salahiyatein ataa ki hain. Jahan tak aapki fikr ka talluq hai woh band ke bayaan-par munhasir hai.

---

* Film-maker Subhash Ghai would later corroborate the fact the geetkar had exactly this sort of attitude towards his work.
† Subhash Ghai would confirm this claim too.

Mutalba bhi nihayat hi zaroori cheez hai, alfaaz ka intekhaab aur un ki nashist mein sher ki asar-angezi ka raaz muzmar hai. Khuda aapko urdu shairi ka qabil-e-fakhr shayar hone ka maqaam ata farmaaye.

Duago
Bismil Saeedi, Delhi

Translation:

Dearest, respected and dignified Anand Prakash Saheb Bakhshi!

God has blessed and bestowed you with good poetic abilities and skills. As far as your, a poet's, imagination is concerned, it will depend on the emotions being expressed in a verse. Your thought process is very high. Life experiences are important for writing poetry. Continual reading and study of poetry and stories are equally necessary; moreover, the selection of words and their arrangement in verse are key to making your writing apt and impressive. The secret of writing an impressive and expressive verse is hidden in the choice of words and their arrangement. May God bless you with a place of pride and honour in the world of Urdu shayari.

My blessings are upon you.
Your well-wisher.

What encouraged Bakhshi the most at this stage in his life, when he had decided to leave the army but hadn't yet put in his papers, was the compliment Saeedi had paid him: '*Azeezi-o-Muhibbi Bakhshi, tumko Farsi nahin aati, lekin tumhari tabiyat mein Farsi hai, tumhare mizaaj mein Farsi hai, aur yeh tumhaare bahut kaam aayegi* (Dear Bakhshi, you don't know Farsi, but Farsi is in your soul, Farsi is in your temperament, and this would stand you in good stead).'

Way before he was to knock on the doors of film-makers, this was by far the best compliment a renowned poet had ever paid him.

* * *

A (Final) Farewell to Arms

On 27 August 1956, Anand Prakash Bakhshi took voluntary discharge from the army, for his second determined attempt at making it as a songwriter in Bombay. In total, he had served the Indian Army for eight years and, prior to that, the Royal Indian Navy for two years.

Around September 1956, he arrived in Bombay for the second time as an ex-fauji armed with Captain Varma's recommendation letter. He had a manuscript of sixty poems with him, as well the moral support and encouragement of his comrades, seniors and, most importantly, his mentor Bismil Saeedi. He was uncertain but determined, looking forward to what colours life would bring to his path this second time.

Bakhshi's wife, Kamla, had resided with her in-laws in Delhi for about four years after the marriage. In 1958, she shifted to her maternal home with their first-born. Bakhshi thought it was for the best, as his own family was against his decision to leave the army the second time, and had she stayed back she would possibly have faced some heat in his absence. Though his father-in-law, Amar Singh Mohan, was as much against his decision to leave the army as his family, Bakhshi felt his wife and their daughter will be cared for and supported best at her maternal home.

Amar Singh, who had retired by 1958 and was living on a pension, was horrified and disgusted by his son-in-law's rash and careless decision to leave his wife and just-born daughter for an insecure career in films! He, too, was a Mohyal and could not fathom, all through the next decade, why a Mohyal fauji who'd just had a baby would leave his job and send his wife to her maternal home (even if temporarily) for a career in films. Though he did send some money to Bakhshi in Bombay a couple of times, during emergencies, he would severely admonish him in all their written correspondence. There came a time when he refused to send Bakhshi even a rupee as further support.

Dad would later admit to us that he did risk his family for his dream, but that was another reason why he gave us more than his best when he eventually made it as a geetkar. No plan B.

'Zamane mein aji aise kai nadaan hote hain, wahan le jaate hain kashti jahaan toofan hote hain'

—*Jeevan Mrityu*

6

1956–1959

'Zindagi Har Qadam Ek Nayi Jung Hai'

In 1956, Anand Prakash Bakhshi made his second attempt at trying his luck in Bombay knowing the challenges that lay ahead. 'Either I'll become an artist or I'll drive a taxi. But I won't go back without a respectable livelihood.' He already had a driving licence, as he had driven transportation trucks during his training in the army meant for military and commercial use. He thought driving a taxi could become his part-time occupation, a means to sustain his life in Bombay till he found a job in films. 'I had no other educational qualification nor family support to fall back on so I had to work at it harder than others'

The first place Bakhshi stayed at was the passengers' waiting room at the Dadar railway station. A few days later, he rented a room at Dadar Guest House, Tulsi Pipe Road, after which he shifted to Hotel Evergreen (later known as Hotel Guru) in Khar West. He would spend all his time writing songs. The hotel was close to the houses of some established music composers—S.D. Burman was in Khar and Roshan in Santacruz. Pandit Hariprasad Chaurasia and his wife were also guests at Hotel Evergreen and would leave daily to look for work. Bakhshi would talk less, write more, and he would sometimes entertain those around him by singing his poems and songs. He would have his meals at a sweet shop nearby and eat paans.

The person cleaning his room always complained that Bakhshi threw a lot of paper away with his hand-written Urdu notes and that he ate lots of paans!

Living a bachelor's life in Bombay, he would finish his dinner and begin writing. He wrote standing under a street lamp outside a sweet shop near the Khar station. The owner of the sweet shop was fond of poetry and soon struck up a friendship with Bakhshi. After a few months, he confided in him, 'Bakhshi, *dekho*, I like your poems and I like you. So I will tell you something I don't want you sharing with anyone. We put blotting paper in our rabdi to make it thicker. I know you are very fond of rabdi, but I don't want to deceive you. So don't eat our rabdi.'

Back in the 1950s, when he first arrived in Bombay, it had been difficult for him to make a breakthrough. Writers, composers and film-makers worked in set teams; they had their own favourites and did not want to 'experiment' with newcomers. Film-making is expensive and film-makers, in my own experience too, are very superstitious. They pursue hits often blindly and shun people associated with flops as blindly. In the '50s and '60s, music composers and lyricists were a very close-knit group, and a newcomer could not easily get the attention of the composers. Bakhshi made it a point to meet three or four people daily to ask for work. He would also visit film studios— like the Famous Studios in Mahalaxmi, Kardar Studios in Dadar and Filmistaan in Goregaon among others—every day. A few composers did not take him seriously as a writer when they felt that he wanted to be a singer too and that may have worked against him.

Anuradha Roy, the wife of Hariprasad Chaurasia, told me, 'In the late '50s or early '60s, Bakshiji was staying in the same guest house (Evergreen Hotel, Khar Station Road, Khar West), that my husband, Hariji, and I were staying at. His family lived in Lucknow, I was told. And he lived here on his own as he could not afford to bring them to Bombay. We had rooms on the same floor, so when I would pass his room I would often encounter the sweeper complaining that he had found too many crumpled papers in Bakshiji's room. And I wondered what Bakshiji wrote, since he threw away so much paper every day, making the sweeper's job harder. Two decades later, we happened to live in the same residential building in Bandra. We were one floor above his, and every day we would see the best of cars and the best of composers, producers, directors and actors arriving to meet Bakshiji for music sittings. We could hear the music sittings going on in his house until late, up to 9 or 10 p.m. That sweeper had no idea that the guest in his hotel was to one day become such a big lyricist.'

After a few months in Bombay, when he could not find work as a truck driver or car driver, he even pretended to be a motor mechanic and landed a job. But the owner of the car garage soon found out that Bakhshi was not good at the job on the very first day. and told him to leave.

These minor misfortunes aside, Bakhshi was soon to land a film, his first, which he considered his biggest film ever! Far bigger than *Sholay* and *Dilwale Dulhania Le Jayenge* decades later.

* * *

'Meri sabse badi film'

Desperate for a break and scared he would run out of his savings, Bakhshi would visit all the film and song recording studios in Bombay, waiting for long hours to meet any film-maker or composer he could run into. The ex-fauji strategized it all like a war drill, aiming to meet at least five people daily before returning to his room.

During one such strategized visit, he was waiting outside the office of actor Bhagwan Dada (Bhagwan Abhaji Palav) at Ranjit Studios. Bhagwan Dada was a star actor in those days, working on his directorial venture *Bhala Admi*, produced by Brij Mohan. Bakhshi befriended the 'office boy' and found out that Bhagwan Dada was stressed about his lyricist not having turned up for a song sitting that day and was looking for a replacement. Bakhshi seized the moment and 'encountered' Bhagwan Dada—by barging straight into his cabin to ask for work!

Bhagwan Dada was taken by surprise and asked him what he wanted. Bakhshi said he was a songwriter looking for work. Bhagwan Dada said, 'Let's see if you can write a song.' He then narrated the story of the film to Bakhshi and gave him fifteen days to write the song.

Within fifteen days, Bakhshi had managed to write the lyrics of four songs. It was not a difficult task for him, because in his army days he would rewrite all the songs, in his own words, of some of the films he'd enjoyed watching. Bhagwan Dada liked all the four songs and signed him as the second lyricist of the film. It was an action film, something Nand had loved watching in his formative years.

He was paid Rs 150 for these four songs. The first one—'*Dharti ke lal, na kar itna malal, dharti tere liye, tu dharti ke liye*'—was recorded on 9 November 1956. The music composer was Nisar Bazmi who a few years later migrated to Pakistan.

Within two months of his second stint in Bombay, the geetkar had been finally born. 'I thought I'd conquered the world! I thought all my problems were over. Little did I realize that they'd only just begun!' The film took two years to complete, was a box-office failure and went unnoticed. So did Bakhshi. For the next six years, he did not have much work in the movie industry. He said, 'You either have no work or you have too much of work. I have experienced both. I was blessed that I experienced the former only in the first eight years of my career.'

A decade later, a few months after the success of *Jab Jab Phool Khile* in 1965, Bhagwan Dada happened to meet the geetkar Anand Bakshi at a film party. He was going through a low phase in his career as an actor and advised him, 'Anand Bakshi Sahib, *khushi ki baat hai, aap ka bahot naam ho gaya hai. Magar ek baat yaad rakhna, ke yahan iss duniya mein aadmi ko naam se zyada us ka kaam zinda rakhta hai*

(It's great to know that you've made a name for yourself. But always remember that what a man needs to survive in this world is good work rather than just a name).' As Dad told us, 'I never ever forgot those golden words from my first benefactor in the industry.'

Bhala Admi was released in 1958, two years after the songs had been recorded. Bakhshi had still not found work in films. He was writing a song or two every few months; for some of these he received payment but his name was not credited.

'When I saw my name in the credits, I cried in happiness. Today, if I am called a successful writer, it is because of Bhagwan Dada. A star actor and producer giving me work was a validation of my dreams, prayers and hopes. *Bhala Admi* was released in 1958 and did not do well at the box office, nor were the songs popular; so it did nothing for my career, *lekin phir bhi, mere liye woh hamesha meri sabse badi film hai aur hamesha rahegi. Kyunki uss film ne hi toh ek geetkar ko iss duniya mein janam diya* (. . . and yet, for me, it will always be my biggest film. Because it was that film that brought the lyricist into this world).'

In his copy of the newsprint poster of the film, he has underlined his name in red ink. How excited he was! On this poster, his surname was spelt as 'Bakshi' instead of Bakhshi, and the misspelling stuck. He didn't care, because his priorities were different. In his own words, 'I am just looking for another chance to write.' This was his life's philosophy from 1950 all the way to 2002.

After recording his first four songs in 1956, he found no work until 1959. He used to say that this was among the most difficult phases of his life in Bombay. He was running out of patience, because he was running out of his savings and his family back home was cursing him for leaving the pension wali army job. Once again, he wrote a personal statement, this time in the form of a poem, titled 'Woh Tadbeerien Nahi Hoti', to inspire himself. It was published more than two decades later, in 1980, in *Ruby* magazine, New Delhi.

Seeing that Bakhshi could not find work even after the release of *Bhala Admi*, someone told him that he should return to the army.

'The army needs you, the film industry does not,' Bakhshi was told. But this remark, thrown at him like a rock, only galvanized the fauji in him to try harder and show 'them' that they were all wrong. Bakhshi used every stone thrown at him to make the path he walked sturdier and to build the castle of his childhood dreams. *'Ek din mere gaane radio pe bajenge* (One day, my songs would play on the radio)'. The first time he happened to hear his song on the radio, it was in a bazaar, in 1959. The song was *'Chunnu patang ko keheta hai kite, wrong hai ya right'*, from *Zameen Ke Tare*.

He was now nearly out of money. Even his father-in-law, who had supported him on and off for two years by sending him small amounts from Lucknow, refused to help him any more and demanded that his son-in-law abandon his foolish dream, return to his reputed family in Delhi and look for some respectable work once again.

* * *

Bhala aadmi

Bhagwan Dada was the first *bhala aadmi* (kind soul) who gave Anand Bakhshi his break in films in 1956. Bakhshi had walked into his office and asked for a chance to write. Nearly two years later—the film *Bhala Admi* had not yet released—Bakhshi had a chance encounter with another bhala aadmi, at the Marine Lines railway station—a place he would sometimes visit to write poems.

Dejected, disappointed, disillusioned a second time from life in Bombay, he had never faced such rejection and humiliation as a fauji among civilians, a hopeless Bakhshi was quite aimlessly sitting at the Marine Lines station, writing down his thoughts and contemplating his immediate return home, a defeated soldier-poet. He was approached by a Western Railway ticket checker, who asked him to show him a valid travel ticket. Bakhshi had none. He was asked to pay a fine for loitering. Bakhshi had no money for the penalty. The ticket checker noticed that Bakhshi had written some Urdu verses in his notebook and questioned him about it. Coincidentally, the ticket checker was a lover of poetry and on finding out that this ticketless man was writing poems, he asked him to narrate what he had written and even sat down beside him to hear more closely. He was impressed by Bakhshi's writing and asked him to recite some more. He liked all that he heard.

He asked the poet, 'What are you doing here?' Bakhshi felt at ease telling him all about his family's journey as refugees from Pindi to Delhi and about his second attempt to make it in Bombay as a film artist. The ticket collector, strangely, treated him to tea and samosa. By the time they finished their snack, the ticket collector, straight out of the blue, offered, 'Bakhshi, you write well. You must not go back. Stay here in Bombay. I am certain you will get a break. Your writing is as good as the film writers who are big names today.'

On learning Bakhshi had no money to stay back in the city—his father and father-in-law having refused to support him any longer—the ticket checker suggested, 'I live alone in Borivali. My family lives in Agra. It gets lonely, and I would like the company of a poet. You stay with me, and I don't want any rent from you. You narrate your poems to me. When you get work, you can look for your own accommodation.' That very day, in May 1958, the ticket collector Chhitar Mal Swaroop took Bakhshi, a stranger, to his house at 24H, Jawala Estate, S.V. Road, Borivali West, Bombay.

He kept this stranger at his home for the next three to four years! Never charged him a rupee and never asked him for any favour all his life. He would even give him pocket money of Rs 2 daily, to eat and travel, to see producers and directors and ask them for work. He would sometimes slip a rupee or two into Bakhshi's empty wallet, so that the latter would not feel humiliated asking for money. Bakhshi said, 'I never asked nor found out why he helped me without charging me or asking me to ever pay him back when I got established. He was a *farishta* (an angel) that my Bansi Wale sent to help me during the worst period of my life.'

Chhitar Mal Uncle would visit us nearly thrice a year. He always brought Agra *ka petha* for Dad and us. I never heard my dad address anyone in his life as 'Ustaad' except Chhitar Mal uncle. He addressed Dad as 'Bakshiji'. In the late '90s, my father tried to pay back the debt he felt he owed his Ustaad. He offered to finance any possible business ideas Chhitar Mal Uncle might have in mind post his retirement from the railways at the age of 60. Ustaad Chhitar Mal told his dear friend on his face, 'I am not interested in setting up any kind of business for myself after retiring. Don't make me a proposition like this ever again. I have never hinted nor expected anything in return from you for whatever you think I did for you back then. It was our destiny that we met. Nothing more to it.'

So, I believe, Anand Bakshi had two mothers, one who gave him birth, Sumitra Bali, and the second, Ustaad Chhitar Mal. 'Had Chhitar Mal not stopped me from returning to Delhi or to the army, I, a married man, with a two-year-old baby, would have gone back home and would not have had the means, the will or the courage to make a third attempt.' This bhala aadmi was responsible for every single film opportunity that arrived on Anand Bakhshi's path until he passed away in 2002. Chhitar Mal Uncle passed away in 2001.

Sheltered by Chhitar Mal Swaroop, Bakhshi finally found the temporary stability he needed in an alien city. The struggle for work went on for another year, until Bakhshi met the renowned music director Roshan. Meeting Roshan was another turning point in his early years here because they were to create Bakhshi's first two hit songs. The other star composer he met during this most challenging period was S. Mohinder (Mohinder Singh); they were to do many films together and become great friends. Mohinderji recounted this incident to me four years ago, 'One day, your daddy and I had had a lot to drink, and he was refusing to call it a night, refusing to catch the local train that would take him home. I had gone to the station to see him off. On the platform, I kept pleading that he must get on the next local train and head home, but he wanted to hang out some more. *"Chal mere bhai, tere haath jodhta hoon, paun padhta hoon, chal mere bhai ab train pe chadh ja."* He used that line in a song he wrote, featuring Rishi Kapoor and Amitabh Bachchan, for *Naseeb*, nearly two decades later. When I heard the song, I laughed aloud, remembering our drinking and Mughlai food sessions together post some great song recordings.'

* * *

'Rasta bana le apna'

Roshan Lal Nagrath was among the top music composers in the '50s. After many failed attempts at meeting successful composers, Bakhshi met Roshan sometime in 1959, at the Filmistan Studios in Goregaon. Nagrath accepted Bakhshi's pitch as a songwriter and asked him to come over to his house in Santacruz and recite his poems. However, as the date approached, Roshan Sa'ab cancelled the meeting. This happened three or four times over the next few weeks. This made Bakhshi even more desperate to meet him and narrate his poems to him. Roshan Sa'ab was a sought-after composer and was very busy. One day, he gave Bakhshi an appointed: *'Bakhshi, tum na aisa karo, kal subha dus baje mere ghar par aa jana. Tumhare gaane sununga* (Bakhshi, do one thing, come to my house tomorrow morning at ten. I will hear your songs).'

A thrilled Bakhshi returned to his place of residence in Borivali and prayed that this meeting would not get cancelled once again. That night, it rained so much that it seemed to Bakhshi the city would drown by morning. The local trains and BEST busses had stopped plying. The city had been flooded. At dawn, Bakhshi feared that the rain was trying to stop him from meeting Roshan Sa'ab, that destiny was conspiring against him. But he considered himself a fauji, and with his training behind him, he decided that he would not let the enemy (be it rain or destiny) win today.

The ex-fauji strategized, calculating that it would take him at least three hours to walk from Borivali West to Roshan Sa'ab's residence in Santacruz West. Walking was no big deal for the ex-infantry man. Army had trained him to jog long distances. He set out four hours ahead of the appointed time of 10 a.m. He covered his writing diary with his bath towel, took an umbrella and started walking to Santacruz in the stormy rain.

He reached Santacruz before the appointed time! That habit remained with him through the decades. The film-maker Subhash Ghai told me, 'Your daddy's best quality was not his ability to write profound thoughts in simple, everyday words, but his discipline and respect for time. He never delayed a single song I asked him to write.'

Back to Bakhshi in1959. His umbrella had broken, his leather slippers had given way and his diary was damp with rainwater. Yet, he was delighted to see that the pages and the words he had written were intact. He had used the broken umbrella to shield his diary from the rain and had succeeded. This dairy had the sixty poems he had carried with him when he arrived for the second time to his *sapno ki nagri Bambai*.

He had walked some nineteen kilometres. Standing at the door of Roshan Sa'ab's house, he rang the bell. When Roshan Sa'ab saw the drenched Bakhshi, he remarked, '*Arre Bakshi, tum aadmi ho ya bhoot? Tum aisi toofani barsaat mein kyun aaye? Tumhara aana itna zaroori nahi tha* (Are you a man or ghost? Why did you come here in this heavy rain? It wasn't necessary).'

'*Aap ne mujhe bulaya tha aaj das baje, meri kavitaein sunne ke liye* (You had called me today at ten, to listen to my poems)!'

'*Haan, bulaya toh tha. Magar kaam itna zaroori nahin tha* (Yes, I did invite you, but it wasn't this important).'

'*Sa'ab, aap ke liye zaroori na ho, magar mere liye aap ka meri kavita sunna bahot zaroori tha* (Sir, maybe it wasn't important for you, but to get you to listen to my poems was very important to me).'

Impressed by Bakhshi's passion, Roshan Sa'ab gave him a break as songwriter in *C.I.D. Girl* (1959). This was a turning point in Bakhshi's life. His first song with Roshan Sa'ab became a hit. In fact, his first two hit songs were from this film. The two went on to work together in many films: *Maine Jeena Seekh Liya* (1959), *Warrant* (1961), *Vallah Kya Baat Hai* (1962), *Commercial Pilot Officer* (1963), *Bedaag* (1965) and *Devar* (1966).

Now that a big composer like Roshan Sa'ab had worked with the newbie Anand Bakhshi, some other composers, too, began to offer him work. But the ruling composers of those days were still unaware of him. Many years later, when Roshan Sa'ab's son Rajesh Roshan started his music career, Anand Bakshi was among the top songwriters in the country, and this time it was Roshan Sa'ab's son, Rajesh, who was the newbie. The film was *Julie* (1975), for which Anand Bakshi wrote the lyrics and Rajesh Roshan composed the music. The film's songs—including *'Bhool gaya sab kuch, yaad nahi ab kuch'* and *'Dil kya kare jab kisi ko, kisi se pyar ho jaye'*—are popular even today.

Though geetkar Anand Bakshi was now getting some work—doing one or two film songs a year—he was still unable to provide for his family in Lucknow. He began looking for acting jobs as an 'extra' and did the rounds of the studios, looking for work as an actor or a lyricist. *'Jo bhi kaam mile, bhagwaan ka prasaad* (Whatever work I get would be a godsend). I would ask my friends, and even the music composer Mohinder Singhji, whom I had worked with, for acting jobs when I needed money. In 1966, I acted as a fakir lip syncing a song in a film called *Picnic.'*

At Kamla's maternal home in Lucknow, Bakhshi's father-in-law, Amar Singh Mohan, now a retired subedar living on his army pension, was deeply disappointed that the son of an illustrious Pindi family was wasting precious money, time and youth in Bombay, trying for a film career, having already left a secure army job. Moreover, Bakhshi had left his wife and child in their care, abdicating his dharma towards his family for an illusion.

In 1959, Amar Singh wrote to his son-in-law, asking him to take his wife, Kamla, and daughter, Suman, from their home in Lucknow and keep them in Bombay with him. Amar Singh told him, in his commanding tone, that it was his duty as a husband to be with his wife!

'In 1958, Kamla enrolled herself in a professional course, at the Industrial Training Institute, Lucknow, to qualify in the cutting and tailoring trade in order to support her personal expenses. For at least three to four years, I could not afford to visit them in Lucknow. I felt humiliated that I had not as yet found work as a writer to support my family. My eldest daughter lived her childhood and teens during my worst financial period. She will always be my favourite child of the four.

'Kamla and her parents were very angry with me for my negligence towards my family. When I visited them around 1960, after a gap of about three years, my daughter, Suman, did not recognize me and asked Kamla if I was her daddy. Kamla said angrily, "He is not your daddy. He is a stranger who has come to visit us." I was able to stand tall as a lyricist for four decades due to the unconditional support Kamla gave me. She is the pillar of my career and our family.

'I always regretted the cost my family had to pay in the early years of our marriage, with my wife, along with our daughter, having to live with her parents, thanks to my passion to be in films. I missed them and would often look at their photos, as I could not afford to visit them or call them over or speak to them through expensive STD calls.

'I wrote songs because it was a passion more than a profession. But I was desperate to earn money from it, so that my family would not pay a heavy price for my passion. My anger at not being recognized for my talent and my frustration at not finding any work or income made me even more determined, not just to succeed financially but to be the winner, to be the best lyricist. In the army, our commanding officer would motivate us while training using these words, "There are no runners-up in the army. Either you kill the enemy or become their prisoner. You have to be No. 1, the winner." I was able to bring my wife, daughter and first son to live with me in Bombay on 13 May 1963. I etched this date in my diary; that is how much it meant to me. To have them with me while I wrote . . . All my life, I always wrote from my bedroom, sitting on my bed. I never needed a desk. Nor did I ever ask for a room at some hotel to write. My producers loved me as I saved them money.'

Dad would rarely make us listen to his lyrics while writing. Sometimes he would sing to Mom the lyrics of some romantic song he had been penning. She would spend a lot of her time in his bedroom, doing her own stuff. He always wanted her or one of us to be home. He sometimes felt anxious if none of us were around. There were days when I would get upset with him for making me stay home for no reason, when no one else was around. Only after he passed away, and I became privy to his personal diary, did I realize that he suffered from the anxiety of being alone. I wish I had understood my daddy better.

7

1959–1967

Kaagaz Kalam Dawaat: Inking His Way to the Top

It is difficult to capture Bakhshi's journey in a linear fashion from here onwards. I wanted to cover things about his early life in films and on the home front that have not yet been touched upon—insights that mostly his family, close friends and a few passionate fans were privy to. This chapter is a collection of his milestone songs, and some anecdotes related to them, from the first decade of his work, before he went on to play an innings with nearly ninety-five music composers and 250 directors.

The 'Pindiwala boy' with a dream, Nand gained immense popularity only 1962 onwards as Anand Bakshi. His songs were played on radio shows like *Binaca Geet Mala* day after day, week after week. And this went on for nearly forty years. (The show was hosted by Ameen Sayani and was, for almost five decades, considered India's No. 1 song-countdown show.) But Anand Bakshi himself maintained a list of his hit songs. These were the forty-odd songs he wrote between the years 1959 and 1967 that were considered 'hit' and 'popular' back then.

I present these songs, which he mentioned in his handwritten notes. Next to each song title, he meticulously jotted down the date of the recording, and the names of the music director and singer.

To me, this signifies the importance he gave to his team, to the singer and composer. He stopped writing these notes when asthma began to overwhelm him, around 2001. The list I present here is limited, but it showcases his slow and steady rise to the top over a period of eight to nine years.

* * *

1959

1. 'Badi buland meri bhabhi ki pasand, par kum nahi kuch bhaiya bhi, kya jodi hai'—C.I.D. Girl (1959); music by Roshan

'Badi Buland' was his first *popular* song as well as his first song with the music composer Roshan. This was the beginning of Bakhshi's career as writer, and in spite of having had a box-office failure associated with his name, he happened to get work with a star singer like Mohammed Rafi. Though he lacked regular work for about three years on his arrival in Bombay, time and luck seemed to have been on his side. Roshan Sa'ab was a well-established composer when Bakhshi began to pursue him, persistently, for just one chance at least.

'The fact that I had come to meet Roshan Sa'ab in the stormy rain, to narrate my poems, made him decide to give me a hearing. He liked what I recited and gave me work. After this, I kept getting work on and off. So this was like a turning point for me in my days of struggle. Yet, I did not find work to my satisfaction, nor money to bring my family over from Lucknow. Over the next three years, I would get a song or two to write now and then, and this went on until my next big break, with the movie *Mehndi Lagi Mere Haath*, in which I got the chance to write all the songs. The movie was a hit too.'

'Badi Buland' was recorded on 4 July 1958 and was sung by Mohammed Rafi. A verse from this song goes, 'Sajega dulha sehere se, dulhan sajegi ghunghat se, padhenge mantar punditji, phere padenge jhat *pat se.'* It encapsulates, in only a few words, the characters' culture, the tradition of marriage and the couple's excitement to get married. From the beginning of his career, Anand Bakshi was a true film lyricist, engrossed and inspired by the story, screenplay and characters. His second popular song was also from the same film, *C.I.D. Girl*.

2.   *'Haye, dard-e-dil, zara zara, deta hai ji bada maza, hans ke le, jisse mile, halka sa, thoda sa'*

Anand Bakshi teases the legends of love in this song: *'Romeo–Juliet, Laila–Majnu, Shirin aur Farhaad, arre aise kitne naam meri jaan, hongey tum ko yaad, bhari jawaani, issi ki khaatir, kar gaye jo barbaad.'*

* * *

1960

3.   *'Chunnu patang ko kehata hai kite, bolo beta tingu, yeh wrong hai ya right?'*—*Zameen Ke Taare* (1960); music by S. Mohinder

S. Mohinder (Mohinder Singh) was another established composer back then. In this song, Anand Bakshi conveys how a child (played by Honey Irani, mother of Zoya and Farhan Akhtar) is playfully testing the English vocabulary of his younger sibling while teaching him what's right and wrong. The riddles are rooted in their locality and culture. This was the first song of his that he heard playing on the radio, fulfilling one of his childhood dreams: *'Ek din mere bhi gaane radio pe bajenge.'*

* * *

1961

4.   *'Honton pe hansi, palkon pe haya, ankhon mein shararat, rehati hai'*—*Warrant* (1961); music by Roshan

This was his first 'hit' song. It was sung by Lata Mangeshkar and was recorded on 6 November 1959. She, too, was a star singer then. In this song, Anand Bakshi describes the depth in the captivating eyes of the film's beautiful female protagonist, '*Jhaanko toh nasheeli ankhon mein, dekho toh zara, sagar ki bhala, phir kisko zaroorat, rehti hai.*'

The year 1961 was also when his second child, a son, was born. Gogi (Rajesh) was born on 13 September at 4.30 p.m. in Lucknow. Gogi, too, seemed to have brought good luck to his father's life, because Anand Bakshi's first hit film, in which all songs were written by him, arrived the very next year. (There is one more hit song from this year, which he forgot to note, from *Razia Sultana*, 'Dhalti Jaye Raat', music by Lachhiram.)

* * *

1962

5. '*Mehndi lagi mere haath re*'—*Mehndi Lagi Mere Haath* (1962); music by Kalyanji–Anandji (KA). His first film with KA. They went on to work on 34 films.

This film was directed by Suraj Prakash, who went on to direct Anand Bakshi's first superhit film (across India), *Jab Jab Phool Khile*, in 1965. In the song, Bakshi describes the excitement of a bride beautifully in this verse, '*Kar ke chunariya, sar pe na thehere, dil dhadke din raat re.*'

6. '*Kankariya maare, karke ishare, balma bada beimaan, khud ko has aaya, humko rulaya, balma bada beimaan*'
7. '*Aap ne yun hi dillagi ki thi, hum toh dil ki lagi samajh baithe. Aap ne bhi humme na samjhaya, aap bhi toh hansi samajh baithe. Kya hua, aap ne na pehechana, aur humme ajnabi samajh baithe. Jal raha tha, woh dil humara hi, hum jisse chandni samajh baithe*'
8. '*Teri woh chal hai ke tauba, asia kamaal hai ke tauba, mera woh haal hai ke tauba . . . Teri har adaa, mastani, meri har nigaah deewani*'

How did Anand Bakshi land this film, in which all songs were by him and which became a huge box-office success? It was thanks to his friend and Mohyal relative, the star actor-director-producer Sunil Dutt. 'In this industry, no one helps anyone,' Sunil Dutt had told him. 'Yet I will give you a recommendation letter to meet Raj Kapoor, even though Raj Kapoor works with Shailendra. But you try your luck.' When I joined the film profession in 1998, Dad told me, 'Here, you have to write your own biography.' I used his quote as the dedication of my first book as author *Directors' Diaries*.

It was 1959. Hiren Khera, the first-time producer of the 1961 hit *Mehndi Lagi Mere Haath*, was Raj Kapoor's secretary at that time. When Raj Kapoor met Anand Bakshi, he told Bakshi that he preferred working with Shailendra as they were a well-established team. Before their meeting, while Bakshi was waiting to see Raj Kapoor in his office, he had narrated his poems to Hiren Khera. Khera, who liked to read poetry as a hobby, loved the poems and promised Bakshi that the day he becomes producer he will sign Bakshi for his first film.

Over time, Anand Bakshi, Hiren Khera and Laxmikant–Pyarelal became friends. All four were still 'strugglers' in the industry, yet to arrive on the horizon. They would travel to Khera's house in Chembur with pao (wheat bread), and Khera would cook daal and sometimes make usal pau, Anand Bakshi's and even Laxmikant–Pyarelal's favourite.

In 1960, when Khera got the chance to produce his first film, he could not sign up his friend Anand Bakshi. Hasrat Jaipuri and D.N. Madhok were the two lyricists for the film. However, for some reason they could not do the film. So Khera then approached Anand Bakshi to write all the songs. The film was a hit and so were four of its six songs. It was also Anand Bakshi's first film with composers Kalyanji–Anandji, who were well established back then. However, his first all-India hit was still four years away, and the all-India blockbuster that made him a household name was six years away.

Three years later, in 1965, Kalyanji–Anandji, Hiren Khera and Anand Bakshi came together once again for *Jab Jab Phool Khile*, and it was to become his first hit across India. All its songs were superhit across the nation! Anand Bakshi had now 'arrived' on the Bombay film industry's horizon.

'*Mehndi Lagi Mere Haath ne mere career ke darwaze khol diye* (The film opened the doors of my career). I had been a very angry man until then. I was angry that no one believed in my talent, not even my family and in-laws. In hindsight, that actually helped me and fuelled me to work very hard. I remained an angry man, out to prove myself right, through the '70s. My family must have suffered because of it. But I channelized the energy of that anger mostly into my work. It's important to use your legitimate anger constructively if you want to achieve anything in this world. It's a very important emotion. I began to relax a bit only when I was able to secure my family financially, in a house I owned, in early 1970. But my hunger or passion to write remained the same and has never diminished. Even today, every song is my next exam, and before every exam I still feel that this time I will fail . . .'

Anand Bakshi was paid Rs 250 for writing the songs of this film. When the film and his songs became a hit, he went to the famous Sher-e-Punjab restaurant at the VT station, to have a treat of his favourite meal, tandoori chicken. When he got off the BEST bus at the VT station, he realized his kurta pocket had been cut and picked. He chased the bus for a few kilometres to catch hold of the pickpocket but failed. He narrated this incident to us to convey how fortunate we were to be born when he was financially established.

In 1980, he wrote, '*Paisa yeh paisa, paisa hai kaisa, nahi koyi aisa, jaisa yeh paisa, ke ho musibat, naa ho musibat.*' (From the film *Karz*.) My elder sister Suman was the only one among us four who saw his 'bad' days, and that's why he said she will always remain his favourite child.

To digress here slightly, to gain a deeper insight into my daddy's life, I want to narrate an incident. I asked my dad, during the last few weeks of his life, when he was physically very weak, due to severe asthma, 'You were different with each of us. You gave me and Rani liberties that you did not allow our two older siblings. Why?' He replied after a long silence, trying to get his best breath into his lungs to respond adequately, 'As a fauji, with every drill I learnt to march better the next time. With every poem I wrote during my army days, I learnt to write a better one. With every song, I learnt to write a better one next time. Similarly, with every child, I learnt how to be a better father. I was not born one, every child made me learn something that I used while bringing up the next one. I did not mean to discriminate. Just as my songs made me a better human over the years, I hope every child I had made me a better father.'

9. 'Gham-e-hasti se begana hota, khudaya kaash main, deewana hota' —Vallah Kya Baat Hai (1962); music by Roshan

Here, Anand Bakshi describes the suffering of the character poignantly. I believe he is expressing his own past suffering and his wish that it had all been a dream, 'Jo dekha hai, suna hai, zindagi mein, woh ban ke dard reh jaata na jee mein; faqat ek khwaab, ek afsana hota.'

10. 'Meri tasveer lekar kya karoge tum, meri tasveer lekar, dil-e-dil jeer le kar, looti jaagir lekar, jaali takdeer lekar . . .'—Kala Samundar (1962); music by N. Datta

This was Anand Bakshi's first qawwali. It went on to become a big hit. The composer N. Datta had asked Anand Bakshi to come over to his house. Datta simply wanted someone to write test lyrics for a qawwali he was composing for a film. The lyrics were going to be eventually written by Sahir Sa'ab. Anand Bakshi wrote the mukhda, 'Meri tasveer lekar kya karoge tum.' Datta composed the tune around the dummy lyrics. Sahir Sa'ab arrived and on hearing the lyrics, he encouraged Bakshi to write further. When he heard the rest of the verses, Sahir

Sa'ab recommended that Anand Bakshi be considered for the film. 'That was yet another act of kindness by the most gracious Sahir Sa'ab, to not feel insecure of a new writer and allow him to write in a film for which he himself had been chosen as the lyricist.'

Eventually, Anand Bakshi wrote five songs for this film. This was in 1962. In praise of Sahir, I must add, that it was Sahir, film-maker Yash Chopra's good friend, who would tell Yashji very often, 'Why do you always work with me? Why don't you take Anand Bakshi? He writes very well.' Yash Chopra and Anand Bakshi came together for *Chandni*, in 1989, only after Sahir passed away.

In this particular qawwali, Bakshi has done a remarkable job. It is written in the question-and-answer format. The male character is playfully demanding to know from the female why she needs a photograph of his. She gives it back to him in equal measure, matching his wit, and in every verse there is a subtext of romance between them. This song is sheer delight. As with any film song, one must watch the film to understand and appreciate the song better.

* * *

1963

11. '*Tumhain husn de ke khuda ne, sitamgar banaya; chalo iss bahane tumhe bhi, khuda yaad aaya, ji aaya*'—*Jab Se Tumhen Dekha Hai* (1963); music by Dattaram

Yet another delightful qawwali, another romantic tussle between the lead pair. And another stroke of good luck. That stars Shashi Kapoor and Shammi Kapoor were featured together for the first time in this song.

12. '*Peehu peehu papihe na bol, paun padhoon main papihe tere, bhed na mere khol; mushkil tha pehle se jina, uss pe aaya saawan ka mahina*'—*Holiday In Bombay* (1963); music by N. Datta

Anand Bakshi expresses in this song the female character's anxiety that everyone would find out her secret, that she is in love, and the arrival of the monsoon is making her pine even more for her beloved. She is addressing her feelings and prayer to the papiha (common hawk-cuckoo) that announces the arrival of monsoon, the season of love.

13. '*Chand aahein bharega, phool dil thaam lenge, husn ki baat chali toh, sab tera naam lenge*'—*Phool Bane Angaare* (1963); music by Kalyanji–Anandji

In this song, Anand Bakshi expresses the beauty of the female character as nature at her best, '*Aisa chehera hai tera, jaise roshan savera, jiss jagah tu nahi hai, uss jagah hai andhera . . . Aankh nazuk si kaliyan, baat misri ki daliyan, honth ganga ke sahil, zulfein jannat ki kaliyan; teri khatir farishtay, sar pe ilzaam lenge . . . Chup na hogi hawa bhi, kuch kahegi ghata bhi, aur mumkin hai tera, zikr kar de khuda bhi; phir toh patthar bhi shaayad, zabt se kaam lengey . . .*'

During the recording of this song, Anand Bakshi got acquainted with Laxmikant–Pyarelal, assistants to Kalyanji–Anandji, on 12 September 1961. This significant date is mentioned in Bakshi's notes. They went on to work together in nearly 303 films!

Apart from songs written in praise of the beloved, he also wrote songs that question why people fall in love. From *Mehboob Ki Mehendi* (1971): '*Jaane kyun log mohabbat, kiya karte hain, dil ke badley dard-e-dil, liya karte hain.*'

There's also a patriotic song in *Phool Bane Angaare* that reflects Anand Prakash Bakhshi's fauji spirit: '*Watan pe jo fida hoga, amar woh naujawaan hoga, rahegi jab talak duniya, yeh afsaana bayan hoga.*' It begins with a heart-rending plea, for the soldier to be ready to sacrifice his life for the motherland: '*Himalay ki bulandii se, suno aawaaz hai aayi, kaho maaon se de bete, kaho beheno se de bhai.*' This song became popular a few years after the film's release, during the Indo–Pak war in 1971.

14. *'Sambhal toh le, dil deewana zara theher jaana, abhi na saamne aana zara theher jaana'*

Composed by Kalyanji–Anandji for *Phool Bane Angaare*, the song was a big hit. In it, Anand Bakshi portrays a female character who is unable to control her excitement at seeing her beloved soon. *'Khushi bhi itni, achaanak, main sehe na paoongi, main apne aap mein, bas aaj rehe na paoongi, jo tumse kehna hai mujhko woh keh na paaungi, main yaad kar loon fasana, zara theher jaana.'*

Anand Bakshi was now confident of supporting his family in Bombay. So he travelled to Lucknow to fetch them. His wife, daughter and son arrived in Bombay on 13 May 1963, and the family checked into room number 26 at Hotel Evergreen in Khar West.

His family had been away from him from 1956 to 1963. So there must have been times when his daughter, son and wife badly missed him. He, too, must have often imagined what they were going through, waiting to see him again. As he wrote in a song for *Taqdeer* (1968), *'Saat samundar paar se, gudiyon ke baazar se, achchi si gudiya laana, gudiya chahe na laana, Papa jaldi aa jana.'* This verse always moves me: *'Tum pardes gaye jab se, bas yeh haal huwa tab se, dil diwaana lagata hai, ghar viraana lagata hai, jhilmil chaand sitaaron ne, darwaazon diwaaron ne, sab ne poochha hai hum se, kab jee chhutega gham se? kab hoga unka aana? Papa jaldi aa jaana.'*

Another song of his that comes to mind right, about his separation from his family and their eventual reunion, is from *Aamne Saamne*: *'Kabhi raat din hum door the, din raat ka ab saath hai, woh bhi itefaaq ki baat thi, yeh bhi itefaaq ki baat hai.'*

I am not aware of the financially challenging times Dad had to go through post-Partition, as he never spoke in detail about those years, except telling us children that he and Mom both had seen very bad days after Partition. But once, I did get an insight into their past financial challenges. It happened sometime in the early '90s. I had just begun working—my own little business. One morning, we were having breakfast and I had not finished the eggs I had ordered. Dad asked me why I had not finished all that was on my plate. I said, 'I am not hungry, and I am in a hurry.' He asked me the price of an egg. I said it must cost 25 or 50 paise a piece. He replied, 'When you four were very small, you and your younger sister were babies, your mother would buy one egg, boil it and divide into four pieces, so that all of you could have good and equal nutrition. She would not buy one for herself. Whatever the price of eggs, more expensive or cheaper, but for us, the price of an egg will always be the price your mom paid to feed you all one egg equally. Never forget that and don't waste food again.' I have never wasted food again. If I eat a pakora fried in oil, I lick the oil off the plate too.

* * *

1964

15. 'Aaj hum ko, hasaye na koi, aaj roney ko jee chahta hai; aur bhi muskuraye na koi, aaj roney ko jee chahta hai; geet honton pe aaye na koi, aaj roney ko jee chahata hai'—Badshah (1964); music by N. Datta

16. 'Mere mehboob qayamat hogi, aaj ruswa, teri galiyon mein mohabbat hogi; meri nazrein to gila karti hain, tere dil ko, bhi sanam tujhse shikayat hogi'—Mr. X in Bombay (1964); music by Laxmikant–Pyarelal

This was his first song with Laxmikant–Pyarelal, recorded on 29 July 1963. Kishore Kumar rated this among his top favourites.

Anand Bakshi conveys the anguish and bitterness caused by the male character's unrequited love. The song is addressed to the beloved: 'Meri tarah tu aahen bhare, tu bhi kisise pyar kare, aur rahe woh tujhse parey, toone o sanam, dhaye hain sitam, toh yeh tu bhool na jaana; ki na tujhse bhi inayat hogi, aaj rusva teri galiyon mein mohabbat hogi.' Moreover, he curses her that she, too, will be denied love one day.

Over the next four decades, many of his songs and films, with new and established music composers, actors, singers, directors and producers, were major hits. Naturally, in an industry that worships the rising sun, many film-makers wanted to work with him.

This was the year of the birth of his third child, Daboo, which is my nickname. I was born on 16 March, Monday, at 10.30 p.m. His second daughter, Rani (Kavita, in his words, *'meri doosri badi kavita'*) was born the next year, 1965. Once again, his Biji's words, that daughters bring great luck to their fathers, proved true. *Jab Jab Phool Khile* was his first resounding success across the country.

* * *

1965

His fourth child, second daughter, Rani (Kavita), was born on Holi, 17 March, Wednesday, at 9.38 p.m. in Bombay.

17. *'Pardesiyon se na akhiyan milana, pardesiyon ko hai ik din jaana'*—
    Jab Jab Phool Khile (1965); music by Kalyanji–Anandji

In the sad version of this song, the male character, feeling betrayed and abandoned, laments, *'Pyar se apne yeh nahi hote, yeh pathar hain, yeh nahi rote, inke liye na ansoon bahana . . . Na yeh baadal, na yeh taare, yeh kagaz ke, phool hain saare, inn phoolon ke na bagh lagana.'*

'My career took off because of the success of "Pardesiyon Se Na Akhiyan Milana". Even Manmohan Desai complimented me when it played on *Chhaya Geet* (Doordarshan) for the first time.'

Anand Bakshi and Manmohan Desai began to collaborate mid-1970s onwards and did exemplary work in seven films, including *Amar Akbar Anthony*.

18. *'Ek tha gul aur ek thi bulbul, dono chaman mein rehete the, hai yeh kahani bilkul sachchi, mere Nana kehete the'*—*Jab Jab Phool Khile*

This song encapsulates nearly the complete story of the film. I like the manner in which Bakhshi authenticates the origins of the fable by mentioning, '. . . *mere Nana kehete the* (as my maternal grandfather used to say).' It reminds me of the many tales Dad would narrate to my nephews and nieces—he was Nana to them—during their annual summer holiday stayovers. He was a fantastic storyteller, and they would be riveted until he slowed down the pace of the drama so they could fall asleep.

19. '*Yeh samaa, samaa hai yeh pyar ka, kissi ke intezaar ka, dil na chura le kahin mera, mausam bahaar ka*'—*Jab Jab Phool Khile*

A verse in this song reminds me of the fauji Anand Prakash Bakhshi's 'masoom sapne', his 'aim in life' of becoming an artist one day. '*Bas ne lage aankhon mein, kuch aise sapne, koi bulaye jaise, naino se apne . . . Yeh sama, sama hai yek ikraar ka, kissi ke intezaar ka . . .*'

20. '*Na na karte pyar tumhi se kar baithe, karna tha inkaar, magar ikraar, tumhi se kar baithe*'—*Jab Jab Phool Khile*

In one of the verses of this song, the female character teases her beloved with affection and a dash of arrogance, '*Koi dil na dega, anaadi anjaan ko, hum ne de diya hai, toh maano ehsaan ko . . .*'

The song 'Yahan Main Ajnabi Hoon' was not as popular as the happier and romantic songs from the same film, yet it received much critical acclaim. In it, Bakhshi expresses the anguish he had felt when he deemed himself a failure in Bombay, twice, and wanted to return to Delhi: '*Nahin dekha, pehele kahin, yeh samaa, ke main bhool se, aa gaya hoon kahan.*' He had written this song as a poem for his own pleasure and later adapted it to the film's story.

All songs of this film were superhits. When I listened to 'Ek Tha Gul Aur Ek Thi Bulbul', I realized for the first time how a song could encapsulate the film's entire story. The next time I heard a film's complete story written in a single song was in 1980. It was a song he wrote for the film *Karz*: '*Ek haseena thi, ek deewana tha, kya umar, kya samaa, kya zamana tha . . .*' As mentioned by Subhash Ghai, he wrote this song within an hour or two, on demand and overnight, as the recording was suddenly scheduled for the next day.

21. '*O dil walon saaz-e-dil pe jhoom lo*'—*Lootera*; music by Laxmikant–Pyarelal
22. '*Humme kya jo harsu ujale huye hain, ke hum toh andheron ke, pale hue hain*'—*Namaste Ji*; music by G.S. Kohli

In this song, Anand Bakshi expresses the plight of being an unfortunate, heartbroken soul who is filled with anguish but is still courageous. '*Kisi aur ka dil jo yun toot jaata, toh shayad khuda se bhi woh rooth jata, humhi hain jo yeh gham, sambhale huye hain.*'

23. '*Chand si mehbooba hogi meri kab, aisa maine socha tha, haan tum bilkul waisi ho, jaisa maine socha tha*'—*Himalay Ki God Mein*; music by Kalyanji–Anandji

Actor Manoj Kumar once told me that this was among his favourite songs. All songs of this film were big hits. In this particular number, Anand Bakshi expresses the male protagonist's joy at having found his dream girl. '*Iss duniya mein, kaun tha aaisa, jaisa maine socha tha, haan tum bilkul waisi ho, jaisa maine socha tha . . . Meri khushiyan hi na baatein, mere gham bhi sehena chahe . . . Aisa hi roop khayalon mein tha, jaisa maine socha tha.*' The song remains popular today and has millions of views on YouTube.

24. '*Tu raat khadi thi chhat pe ki main, samjha ki chaand nikla; bura ho tera tujhe dekh ke kothe se mera pair phisala*'—*Himalay Ki God Mein*

Anand Bakshi himself had grown up in a house in Punjab that had a *kotha*, terrace. This song has the lead pair teasing each other. The male character asks her to express her love for him before he turns old, '*Kat jaae naa meri zindagi, hoe teri kal parason mein.*' The girl teases him back, '*Kal parason mein baat nahi banati, banti hai jaa ke barson mein.*'

25. '*Kankariya maar ke jagaya, kal tu mere sapne mein aaya, balma, tu bada woh hai, zaalima, tu bada woh hai*'—*Himalay Ki God Mein*

In this song, the female character is discreetly conveying that someone has entered her heart and invaded her dreams. Every thought of him distracts her, and yet we can see that she is enjoying the feeling very much.

26. '*Neend nigahon ki, kho jaati hai, kyun ke jawani mein, ho jaati hai, mohabbat, mohabbat, mohabbat; aur mohabbat jo, ho jaati hai, jaan hi jaati hai, toh jaati hai, mohabbat, mohabbat, mohabbat*'—*Lootera*; music by Laxmikant–Pyarelal

There's a verse in this song where Anand Bakshi expresses the pleasant dilemma and detachment from reality we feel when we are in love: '*Duniya se judai ki baatein, guzaari hain kai aisi raatein, jab chaand sitare bhi soye rahe, hum unke khayalon mein khoye rahe; humko jagah ke yeh, soh jaati hai, kyun ki jawani mein, ho jaati hai, mohabbat, mohabbat, mohabbat.*'

27. '*O dil walon saaz-e-dil pe jhoom lo*'—*Lootera*
28. '*Kissi ko pata na, chale baat ka, ke hai aaj wada mullaqat ka, bura haal hai dil ke jazbaat ka, ke hai aaj wada mulakat ka*'—*Lootera*

Anand Bakshi begins this song in his typical style with a nazm, expressing forbidden love. '*Chhupake rakhna mohabbat ko iss zamane se,*

ke aaj saans bhi lena, kisi bahane se.' The female character further
conveys her faith that her lover will come soon to rescue her, *'Mohabbat
ki pyasi mitegi udasi . . . banega fasaana, kissi baat ka, ke hai aaj waada
mulaqat ka.'*

29. *'Sultana sultana, tu na ghabarana, tere mere pyar ko kya, rokega
    zamana, todh ke sab deewarein, tujhe le jayega deewana . . . Shamma
    ussi mehfil mein jalegi jisme hoga parwana'*—*Shreeman Funtoosh*;
    music by Laxmikant–Pyarelal

In this song, Anand Bakshi expresses exactly what the title of one of
his films from the '90s says: *Dilwale Dulhania Le Jayenge'.*

30. *'Pyar ka fasana, bana le dil deewana, kuch tum kaho kuch hum
    kahein; chhoti si hai aaj ki humari mulaqaat, yeh na ho ke jee mein
    rehe jai jee ki baat'*—*Teesra Kaun*; music by R.D. Burman

This was Bakshi's first film with R.D. Burman. The song was recorded
on 24 September 1964. They went on to work on ninety-nine films.

* * *

1966

31. *'Duniya mein aisa kahan, sab ka naseeb hai, koi koi apne piya ke
    kareeb hai'*—*Devar*; music by Roshan

Roshan Sa'ab passed away a year later, in 1967. This song arrived two
years after Anand Bakshi's reunion with his wife and two children,
and by 1966 he had two more children. In a verse, he writes, *'Door
hi rehete hain unse kinare, jinko na koi majhee paar utaare, saath hai
majhee toh kinara bhi kareeb hai, duniya mein aisa kahan sab ka naseeb
hai . . . tu hai toh zindagi ko zindagi naseeb hai.'* He goes on to describe
the blessing it is to have a good life companion, *'Chahey bujha de koi,*

deepak saarey, preet bichhati jaye rahon mein taare, preet deewani ki kahani bhi ajeeb hai.'

32. *'Baharon ne mera chaman loot kar, khizaan ko yeh ilzaam kyun de diya; kissi ne chalo dushmani ki magar, isse dosti naam kyun de diya'*— *Devar*; music by Roshan

Here, the song's protagonist questions why he has been denied love, accusing spring of stripping nature of all her beauty and pinning the blame for the barrenness of winter on autumn. In the last verse, he accuses god: *'Khudaya yahan tere insaaf ke, bahot maine charche sune hain magar, sazaa ki jagah ek khatawaar ko, bhala tune insaaf kyun de diya* (Khuda, I have heard you are fair, yet you allow the guilty to go unpunished).'

33. *'Aayaa hai mujhe phir yaad wo zalim, guzara zamana bachpan ka, haay re akele chhod ke jana, aur na aanaa bachpan ka, ayaa hai mujhe phir yaad vo zalim'*—Devar

I can visualize Dad saying these words to us, speaking of missing his Maaji and his seventeen years in his pind, Pindi, and his wish to visit the place someday.

34. *'Roothe saiyyan, humare saiyyan, kyun roothe, naa toh hum bewafa, naa toh hum jhoote; chain na humein neend na aaye, detey rahey saari raina duhai, koi unki bhi yun hi nindiya loote'*—Devar
35. *'Khat likh de, sanwariya, ke naam babu, kore kagaz pe likh de, salaam babu, woh jaan jayenge, pehchaan jayenge, kaise hoti hai subah se shaam babu'*—*Aaye Din Bahaar Ke*; music by Laxmikant–Pyarelal

In this romantic song, the female protagonist is dictating a letter addressed to her beloved who migrated to the city for work and hasn't yet returned to see her. She wishes that he loses the job that made a slave of him and took him far away from her.

36. *'Yeh kali, jab talak, phool ban ke khile, intezaar, intezaar karo; intezaar woh bhala kya karein, tum jisey, beqaraar, beqaraar karo'*— *Aaye Din Bahaar Ke*

Bakshi expresses the tug of war between two lovers, the man pleading with her to surrender herself to his affection, while she teases him, resisting his invitation, telling him to be patient.

37. *'Suno sajna, papihe ne, kaha sabse, pukaar ke, chaman waalon, sambhal jao, ke aaye din, bahaar ke'*—*Aaye Din Bahaar Ke*

The iconic love song is the female character's declaration, that she has fallen in love, and she tells us that in this blissful moment she can spend eternity. Once again, the lyricist conveys his expression using the papiha bird, whose arrival announces *saawan*: *'Baghon mein padh gaye hain, saawan ke mast jhoole, aisa samaa jo dekha, raahi bhi raah bhoole, ke jee chaha yahin rakh dein, umar saari guzaar ke.'*

38. *'Mere dushman tu meri, dosti ko tarse, mujhe gham dene wale, tu khushi ko tarse'*—*Aaye Din Bahaar Ke*

Anand Bakshi is perhaps the only lyricist who has written a song that's essentially a curse, using references from nature and relationships, yet never crossing over to actually being abusive. Yet again, he begins the song with a nazm, to provide context: *'Mere dil se sitamgar, toone achchi dillagi ki hai, ke banke dost apne doston se dushmani ki hai.'*

He wrote other songs on the theme of friendship as well. This one, from *Sholay*, for instance, bringing enemies together as friends, during the festival of Holi: *'Giley shikwe bhool ke doston, dushman bhi gale mil jaate hain; Holi ke din dil khil jaate hain, rangon mein rang mil jaate hain.'* And this one, from *Dostana:* *'Bane chahe dushman, zamana humara, salaamat rahe, dostana humara.'*

* * *

1967

39. *'Mubarak ho sab ko, sama yeh suhana, main khush hoon mere aansuon pe na jaana, main toh deewana, deewana, deewana'*—*Milan*; music by Laxmikant–Pyarelal

The success of this film's songs across the nation ceased the gossip that Anand Bakshi was a fluke. The film was his first blockbuster. I am glad the film featured Sunil Dutt, as he was the person who, in a way, was responsible for Anand Bakshi's meeting with Raj Kapoor's secretary Hiren Khera back in 1961, who went on to give him the opportunity to write all the songs in *Mehndi Lagi Mere Haath*, which became Bakshi's first hit.

'*Mera sangharsh ka zamana Milan film tak raha. Uske baad mujhe kaam aur paison ki kami nahi rahi. Mere Bansi Wale ne mere masoom sapne poore kiye* (My days of struggle were over after the film *Milan*. I was never short of work and money after that. My Lord Krishna had helped fulfil my innocent dreams).'

My favourite verse in this song is, '*Yeh bole samay ki nadi ka bahaav, yeh babul ki galiyan yeh maajhi ki naav, chali ho toh gori suno bhul jaao, na fir yaad karna, na fir yaad aana, main khush hoon mere aansuon pe na jaana.'*

Post *Milan*, in 1967, when a journalist called on him for an interview, he could not believe it! He asked, 'Are you certain you want to interview me? I am the lyrics writer of the film, not the actor.'

In the words of Pyarelalji, 'Laxmi, and Bakshiji and I came out of Kardar Studios, Parel, after watching the trial show of a Tamil film, which was to be later readapted as *Milan*. We stopped at a paanwallah near Prabhadevi, which Laxmi would regularly patronize. While the paan was being prepared, Bakshiji, who was very happy that we three had come together for this big film, got emotional and said, "*Mubarak ho sabko, sama yeh suhana, main khush hoon mere aansuon pe na jana.*" Later, he used this line in a song for the same film.'

40. '*Saawan ka mahina, pawan kare sor, jiyara re jhoome aise, jaise bann ma nache mor*'—*Milan*

'I thought of the *mukhda* "*Saawan ka mahina, pawan kare sor*" when Laxmikant and I were having paan outside Famous Studios. The paanwallah was taking to someone and again and again saying *sor* and not *shor*. I narrated the mukhda to Laxmikant and he loved it. I wrote the remaining verses soon.

'Which song do I feel was my first hit song? When did I begin to believe that I had "arrived"? A truly popular song is one that travels beyond your city and reaches the villages without any "marketing". It was in the late '60s that people began saying I had arrived. But I did not think too much of their compliments. Until one day, when I was travelling by Frontier Mail from Bombay to Delhi, and at around 2 or 3 a.m. the train stopped in some remote village, at a station lit with kerosene lamps, and here I heard someone sing our song from *Milan*.

'I was surprised. I walked out of the cabin and stood at the train's door to identify the source of that sound in that dark, cold and still winter night. The singer was seated under a large banyan tree at the edge of the station's platform, singing "*Saawan ka mahina pawan kare sor*". It was a fakir seeking alms, playing an instrument made of two wooden plates, hitting them against each other. A poor soul living in an obscure village, which did not even have electricity, was singing our song! It was one of our songs that would help him get a meal or more. Our song was feeding someone somewhere. Moreover, the song had reached this fakir's ears in the heart of our country without any publicity, marketing or film magazine features. I quickly got off the train and handed him some alms and took his blessings. The whistle blew, and I boarded the train running as it was about to leave the platform.

'As that village disappeared in the darkness and the cold winter breeze began to blow against my face, I shut the window. The realization hit me that the sweet people I write for have not just accepted me but embraced me. A fakir, who earned his meals by singing *lok geet* (folk songs), was singing my lyrics, and that was perhaps the biggest reward during my early years in the industry when I was still unsure if my lyrics touch the common man.

'I was a common man before I came to films, and many legends had inspired my journey here. So I wanted to touch the common man's heart with my lyrics. Both lok geet and *lok sangeet* (folk music) have been my inspirations from my childhood days. I have tried to reflect both these forms in my writing across four decades. A touch of the folk spirit is there in many of my lyrics. I have imbibed, primarily, the Punjabi lok geet into my style of writing. If people like my writing, it's because many of my songs were written in the popular Punjabi lok geet style. However, this is not my "I've arrived" moment, because I feel I have yet to write my best song.'

Mukesh and Anand Bakshi expected to win a Filmfare Award for 'Saawan Ka Mahina'. When they didn't win, Bakshi was very disappointed and thought he would never win an award thereafter, because he would never be able to write a better song than this. Dad and Mukesh went to the Sun-n-Sand hotel bar at Juhu post the award ceremony and drowned their disappointment over lots of drinks.

41. '*Raam kare aisa ho jaye, meri nindiya, tohe mil jaaye, main gaoon, tu so jaye*'—Milan

This song reminds me of my childhood, when Dad would sing us to sleep. I can still feel his large yet soft fingers stroking my eyelids. I can hear him whisper a melody, of this song perhaps. I was three when this film was released. I have no clear memory of the words or the *dhun* of the lullabies he sang to us, but I clearly remember the broad and thick fingers of his strong yet nimble hands resting on my little head. The hands that eventually wrote a good part of this book.

42. *'Bol gori bol, tera kaun piya, kaun hai woh jisse tune pyar kiya'—* Milan

Yet another question–answer song by Anand Bakshi. The many songs he wrote in this format, all have a romantic mood. Another such song is from the film *Mera Gaon Mera Desh*: *'Kuch kehata hai yeh saawan, kya kehata hai, shaam saverey dil mein mere kyun rehta hai?'* In 1967, another song of his, 'Bahosh-o-Hawaz', from *Night in London*, received much critical acclaim.

Then came many more box-office super-successes. A few I can name right away, from memory: *Farz* (1967), *Raja Aur Rank* (1968), *Taqdeer* (1968), *Jeene Ki Raah* (1969), *Aradhana* (1969) (the film that inaugurated Rajesh Khanna's road to stardom), *Do Raste* (1969), *Aan Milo Sajna* (1970), *Amar Prem* (1971)—one box-office hit after another. Thereafter, the geetkar Anand Bakshi, thanks to his Bansi Wale Krishna, and his taqdeer and tadbeer, never had to ask for work, until he departed this world in 2002. His aim in life had been achieved. From the mid-'70s onwards, distributors approached with film proposals would often ask producers, *'Iss film mein Anand Bakshi ke geet hain na* (This film has songs by Anand Bakshi, right)?' These milestones in the very first decade of his career, gave Bakshi the respect any writer desires. He was no longer considered just a fluke or a 'tukbandi' writer. Besides, he became a name openly acknowledged and respected even in 'literary circles'.

But there were also those admirers of his who knew the worth of his lyrics as early as 1959. He had begun his career with established music composers like Roshan, S.D. Batish, S. Mohinder and Naushad, and over the next forty-five years, he would end up working with nearly ninety-five music composers in total. He did 303 films with Laxmikant–Pyarelal, ninety-nine with R.D. Burman, thirty-four with Kalyanji–Anandji, fourteen with S.D. Burman, and, decades later, with figures like Nusrat Fateh Ali Khan, A.R. Rahman, etc.

Over a hundred singers have sung his songs. Lata Mangeshkar has sung more of Bakshi's songs than of any other lyricist. Right from the beginning of his career, in the '60s, his songs attracted star singers, like Amirbai Karnataki, Mubarak Begum, Shamshad Begum, Madhubala Jhaveri, Khurshid Bawra, Asha Bhosle, Suman Humrahi Kalyanpur, Sudha Malhotra, Geeta Roy (Dutt), Manna Dey, Mahendra Kapoor, Kishore Kumar and Mukesh, among others.

'I was lucky that I happened to get associated with some star composers, singers, actors, directors and producers. Moreover, those films did well. Nothing succeeds like success here. Our value is determined by box-office success; nothing else matters to film-makers.'

* * *

Three Favourite Composers

S.D. Burman

S.D. Burman was among the top music composers in the '60s. When he was new in Bombay, Bakhshi tried hard to get him to hear his poems.

'Initially, Burman Da did not take me seriously as a writer. He thought I had come to become a singer and that I needed to concentrate on singing alone. I tried innumerable times to meet Burman Da, but he never had time. He was too big and too busy. I understood that, so I would wait outside his house in Khar to meet him.

'One day, Shailendra did not turn up for a song sitting, and Burman Da's assistant told him that I, a brand-new writer, had been wanting to see him. So, Burman Da sent for me. I was elated. I entered

Nand (Anand Bakhshi)
with his Papaji and
Maaji in Hisar, 1936

Nand with his Papaji and
Maaji on the terrace of
their Pindi house, 1930–31

Anand Prakash at the Royal Indian Navy Apprentice Training College, Manora, Karachi, 1944

Anand Prakash's Royal Indian Navy enlistment (1944) and dismissal (1946) orders

Nand's Biji and Bauji during Bauji's posting at the women's jail in Lahore, 1940s

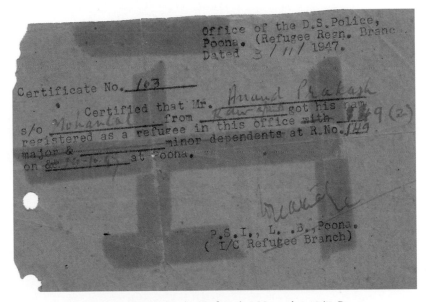

Anand Prakash Bakhshi, the 'Refugee', 3 November 1947, Poona

Anand Prakash Bakhshi while he was training at the Indian Army Corps of Signals, Jubbulpore, 1950; and (*right*) as part of the Corps of Electrical and Mechanical Engineers, Hyderabad, 1956

JUBBULPORE.
24.1.50.

MY AIM IN LIFE.

Every one in this world, rich or poor should have a definet aim in life. A man without any fixed purpose in life is like a ship without radder. Just as the ship is at the mercy of the winds, and is powerless to controle its course.

So a person having no aim in life has nothing by which to guide his actions, or to regulate his conduct.

I, The undersigned, A.P.BAKHSHI.(AZAD.) Intend to study MUSIC. For it is my aim in life to become an ARTIST.   (And to achive that i must join the FILIMS, RADIO, OR THEATERS.)   (TO BECOME SINGER, SONGS COMPOSIOR, MUSIC DIRECTOR, DIRECTOR ect.

A.P.Bakhshi.

(A.P.BAKHSHI.)

God Thanks for fulfilling my dreams
BOMBAY. 10.10.1988
So it happend I became a suceesful song writer. Earned Name
~~fame Money Flats Cars~~ and what not. But somhow on this road
of life I lost my self confidence. I became Anand Bakhshi
from Anand prakash. Now I want to become Anand prakash from
Anand Bakshi. I think I have done it I will do it again.

Bakhshi's 'Aim in Life' note, Jubbulpore, 24 January 1950

Nand's first prayer to his Bansi Wale (Lord Krishna), Mumbai, 1950

Anand Bakhshi's first photo with his pen and *gaano ki kitaab*, Bombay, 1960s

Bakhshi at the Army Bara Khana, the annual event for which he wrote, composed, sang and acted, 1955

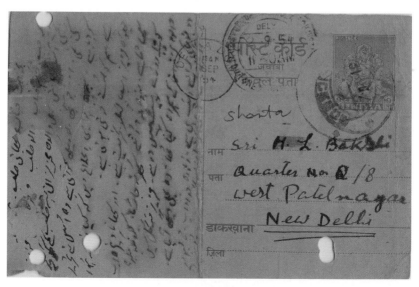

Marriage proposal to Kamla Mohan, written by Bua, 1954

Newsprint ad of *Bhala Admi* (1958), Bakhshi's first film, saved by him

Letter to Bakhshi from his cousin (an Indian Navy officer) about the emotional wounds he suffered after his Maaji's death, 1967

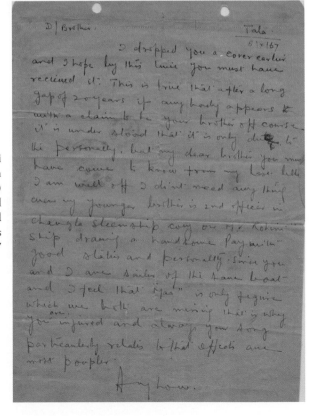

Mukesh, Anand Bakhshi, Lata Mangeshkar and R.D. Burman during a song rehearsal for 'Pyar Ka Fasana', 20 November 1965

Anand Bakhshi, Shashi Kapoor, Hiren Khera, Kalyanji and Anandji, at the silver jubilee celebration of *Mehndi Lagi Mere Haath*, 1962

his house, hopeful and happy that I will finally get to meet him and make him hear my poems too. He asked me to wait a few minutes as he was composing a tune for some film, for which Shailendra was the lyricist.

'I had not even opened my diary when Burman Da's assistant came and said that Shailendra was on his way for his scheduled song-sitting as his other meeting got cancelled. He was to arrive any minute. For some reason, unknown to me then, Burman Da panicked. He told me to run away before Shailendra arrived. Shailendra might feel bad seeing another song sitting going on at a time when he was scheduled to meet Burman Da. Shailendra was a very big lyrics writer then, so I, too, panicked. I, too, felt out of place.

'When I tried to run away from the main door, Burman Da stopped me. He told me not to leave from the main door as Shailendra might see me while walking in. He told me to jump out of the back window! And I did! But I could not climb the high wall of the balcony easily. So Burman Da pushed me over his ground-floor balcony wall!

'Later, in 1964, I did three songs with Burman Da, two of which were sung by Lata Mangeshkar: "Anjaane Mein Inn Hoton Pe" and "Dhan Walon Ka Yeh Zamana". Unfortunately, both these songs were never released. We recorded "Maine Poocha Chand Se", sung by Mohammed Rafi, in 1965. However, the film was not made, and it was his son, R.D. Burman, who would re-record it fourteen years later, in 1979, for Sanjay Khan's *Abdullah* (1980). It was a poem I had written for my own pleasure. In fact, it was among the sixty poems I had arrived in Bombay with, to showcase my talent.

'My first finished film with Burman Da was *Aradhana*, in 1969. The songs were very big hits, and the film established Rajesh Khanna as a star. It was from Burman Da that I learnt a very important lesson, something I had been aware of but he underlined it for me: listen carefully to the film's story narration. The songs you have to write are always in the story. Story *mein gaana hai*.'

One afternoon, Anand Bakshi and his good friend Hari Mehra went to a shop at the Khar station to have paan. On the way home, they saw a beautiful girl walk by. One of them remarked (it's not clear who), '*Wah! Kya roop paya hai.*' Immediately, Anand Bakshi stopped the car under one of the many tall gulmohar trees in Santacruz and told Hari not to speak for about ten minutes. He started penning a song. After *Aradhana* was released, Hari and Bakshi watched the film together. He informed Hari that the song he wrote that day under the shade of the gulmohar trees was S.D. Burman's 'Roop Tera Mastana'.

R. D. Burman

I once asked Dad what he thought R.D. Burman's best quality was. His response was, 'Pancham never got offended if the director or I did not like his tune. He immediately began working on another. He was always willing to make more tunes to our satisfaction. He also accepted and bettered some tunes I suggested or rejected them with equal grace. We had great teamwork.'

They were working on a song for *Hare Krishna Hare Ram* when RD told Dad, 'I like your style of smoking. *Aisa lagta hai aap cigarette nahi pee rahe hain, aap "dum" maar rahe hain* (It looks like you are smoking pot, charas, and not a cigarette).' It was true. Dad would place his cigarette between different fingers at different times, depending on how much smoke he wanted to inhale. Inspiration struck Anand Bakshi. He recollected how some people would say, '*Dum maro aur sab bhool jao* (Smoke up and forget your troubles).' He instantly wrote these words, '*Dum maro dum, mitt jaye gham, bolo subh-o-sham, Hare Krishna Hare Ram.*'

Dev Anand did not want to use this song in the film, because it precedes an inspirational song, '*Dekho o diwano, tum yeh kaam na karo, Ram ka naam badnaam na karo.*' However, RD and Anand Bakshi convinced him to retain it in the film. The rest is history.

During prohibition days in Bombay, RD and Dad would go to a discreet location at Khar Danda to drink cheap country liquor. Both could not afford refined alcohol back then. The police raided the place and they fled the site, only to be confronted by the sea—the facility was located in an abandoned corner of a fishing village. They hid in the marshes all night long, until dawn, and swore never to go back to this joint.

Salim Khan Sa'ab once told me, 'Your daddy was a true friend to RD. Although we were very good friends, he never asked me for any favours or help. The only time he approached me for help was for RD, to recommend him to the producers and directors I knew for work in their films. This was a few months before RD passed away, before the release of his last film, *1942: A Love Story*. For me, that was a sign of your father's good conduct and character, and of their deep friendship.'

Laxmikant–Pyarelal

'My partnership with Laxmi–Pyare worked very well because we understood and respected each other. Most importantly, we gave hits at regular intervals; nothing succeeds like success in this industry. They worship the rising sun. You are only as good as the success of your last film. Even one failure can break bonds of love and friendship that go back years. That is another reason I don't want my children to be a part of this industry.

'Laxmi–Pyare and I understood each other's *mizaaj* (moods) perfectly. Our "tuning" with each other was good, like musical instruments that go well together. So our *jodi* sustained for over three decades and 300-plus films. Moreover, many of those films were box-office successes, and film-makers want to repeat pairs that work. It's a superstitious industry.'

Pyarelal Sharmaji once recounted to me, 'I saw your father for the first time in 1961 during the song recording of Kalyanji–Anandji's film *Phool Bane Angaare* (1963). I was playing the violin in your daddy's song, "Chaand Aahein Bharega". Our first film together was four years later *Mr. X in Bombay* (1964). The song *"Mere mehboob qayamat hogi, aaj ruswa, teri galiyon mein mohabbat hogi"* was a superhit and has since been recreated many times by bands and composers. Honestly, I believe your daddy came to become a music composer and singer, and writing was just his hobby.'

Anand Bakshi was not just inspired by the story of the film to write lyrics; he drew from the spiritual universe within.

8

A Being of Divine Light and Power

Anand Bakshi was once asked if he considered himself the biggest or most popular songwriter from the past three decades, and his reply was,

> 'Main hamesha yeh samajhte aaya hoon ki waqt sabse bada fankaar hai. Wahi humein uthata hai, wahi girata. Issi liye, main hamesha waqt ka mureed raha hoon (I have always believed that time is the greatest artist. It's time that makes us rise and fall. That's why I have always been a fan of time).'

In this chapter, I share with you some of Anand Bakshi's beliefs and ideas about songwriting. Some of these statements have been translated from the original Hindi and Urdu, so the reader will have to excuse whatever is lost in translation. What follows is a slice from a collection of thoughts that spans almost all his professional life. So, let's begin with these lines that he would write on the first page of every new diary of his: 'I am a being of divine light and power. I have access to all that the universe has to offer. I can reach out and take or do whatever I want, whenever I want.'

His lyrics have survived the test of time. And how! There was a time, in the late '50s, when some poets, who were also successful lyricists, looked down upon Anand Bakshi. Even after he became successful and was at the peak of his career, some lyricists from the previous generations considered his writing inferior to their own. 'Anand Bakshi *tukbandi karta hai. Woh toh shayar hi nahi* (He is a rhymester, not a shayar).' Bakshi's response to such put-downs always was, '*I have never claimed to be a poet. Moreover, khayal apna apna, pasand apni apni* (Each to this own).'

The Lyricist: A Breed Apart

The Indian film song bridged the gap between devotional, classical, folk and Western music. Therefore, the same song was loved across different demographics, transcending barriers and boundaries between classes, masses and nations. However, the film lyric is still sometimes considered a poor country cousin of poetry. Exponents of religious songs and shayari once rubbished the film song as profane.

A lyrics writer may not be a special kind of man, but a lyricist is a special kind of poet. The film's story is a necessary component for him or her to work with; it's the story into which the lyrical expression, with its metaphors, poetry and philosophy, has to be weaved. Bakshi was often asked about the source or secret of his success and about the inspiration behind his numerous songs. He would say, as a matter of fact, without any qualms about sharing his secret with his competitors, '*Story sunn ke hi dimaag chalta hai* (My mind starts working only after I have listened to the story). And yes, the *Reader's Digest* monthly inspired me as a writer and a father.'

Many directors told me that before beginning work on a song, Bakshi would ask them to narrate the entire story to him again and again. And once he had absorbed the film's plot, even an earthquake could not have distracted him.

Though the story was of prime importance to him, the lyricist understood and respected the role of the music composer. He knew that it was the trio of composer, singer and lyricist that brought a song together.

These days, singers are often given more importance than the others. On some platforms, the music composers and lyricists are not even credited. A good song must justify the story, reflect the elements of the script. But that rarely happens now. For Bakshi, it was a challenge to write film lyrics, because the writer has to work within the confines of the script, and willingly accept and respect the limited freedom of thought and expression. Of course, the lyrics writer can fly, like a poet. But only within the sky of the story. This makes it a difficult discipline compared to poetry.

Unlike a poet, the film lyrics writer has to gel with the others without losing his or her own individuality.

Pt Narendra Sharma describes the art of the film lyrics with this beautiful statement: 'The film lyrics writer inspires and entertains the listener, encouraging him to believe he or she could perhaps be its writer, its singer, or its music composer.'

Lyrics Writing and More

'Security for my family is my ultimate goal. My New Year resolution was always to see my family happy and settled with work that occupies mind, heart and hands.

'I began writing in childhood as a hobby, subsequently, in adulthood, as a passion and career, and soon after for the financial security of my family, and I continue now because I cannot live without it. Some songs I wrote to run my kitchen, some for my heart. Doing my best for my music composers, film-makers and my family is my *param kartavya* (prime responsibility). After all, I am a hired hand being paid for a job.

'One day, the show will end. My end—every kind of end—is only logical. As I overtook the others, one day some others will overtake me, sweep my fans off their feet with their new or better styles, their words. Life is a chakra that keeps turning. If my songs continue to do well, I am happy. If they don't, it's okay. It's not the end of the world, is it? Poets may write poems for eternity, but I, a lyricist, wrote in accordance with the stories and situations of a particular film. When the story was not inspiring, I had to work even harder to put some *jaan* (life) into my lyrics.

'The rhythms of some of my songs sound like heartbeats. I have written some songs tuned to the metre of my heartbeats. My songs will beat just as our heart beats.

'My songs have taken a toll on my heart. One day, I may not be able to write, or people will not need me any more. But I will leave the industry before it leaves me. Whenever I leave, I will do so as a winner and not a runner-up. I will die with my boots on; that's what we were taught in the fauj.

'I arrived here with lots of disadvantages. I knew no one to begin with, and had no support of my family. However, in hindsight, I now realize that I had one very big advantage: I could sing and suggest Punjabi folk tunes with my lyrics; both came naturally to me. I had been singing and composing my own verses for friends since childhood; I did so for my peers in the army as well. I didn't know then that it was to work to my advantage. Moreover, it was the singing I had been doing since childhood that made me want to write poetry in my teens.

'How do I write film songs? I always first hear the complete story, understand the plot and characters deeply, and then hear the individual situation of the song required. I think I am a very good listener. Good songs exist in good stories. It's a matter of getting them out from the situations itself. I unlock my songs from the situations provided to me by the scriptwriter and director. Then I discuss all I have heard with the music director and director, several times; only after that do we move on, together, to create the tune and lyrics. *Story mein hi gaane hote hain* (The songs are in the story). I always picturize how the song will play on the screen while writing. I can visualize it even if I don't know how the director will shoot it. Film-makers like Subhash Ghai lift my lyrics to extraordinary levels by picturizing them very well.

'Good directors get good songs from me because they inspire me with good stories and sometimes by sharing their own experiences of life. A good director helps me see the song in my head even before I begin writing it. Good directors inspire lyrics writers as well as composers, so they deserve credit for good music too. Good music and good films complement each other. For me, getting the concept clear takes more time than actually writing the song.

'I feed off all these elements—the story, the characterization, even the actor lip-syncing the song and the singer. The rhythms and metres of folk songs are also my inspiration. I heard so much folk and film music during my seventeen years in Pindi that I could very easily compose whatever I wrote. However, the story is my primary and conscious source of inspiration. Everything else—my experiences, etc.—are secondary and subconscious. I have never attempted poetry, shayari, in writing; if it happened, then it was merely organic self-expression that emerged from my subconscious. I whistle or sing along sometimes as I write, *gun-gunate hue likhta hoon*, as it helps me write, and singing my words helps me get the metre right.

'I sometimes suggest the tune to the composers; then it's up to them to use it or not. Sometimes they ask me to sing what I have written and not recite it. That way they get to hear what tune I have in mind for my lyrics. Then they either build on it or reject it. Unlike some other writers, I don't mind writing lyrics to preset tunes; 80 per cent of the time I wrote to preset tunes.

'The advantage of writing to a set tune: it gives the writer a variety of metres to write in. The disadvantage of writing the words first and then setting them to a tune: the song might not be as melodious to sing. The lyrics writer has to maintain a fine balance between the words and the dhun while writing.

'One more advantage I had was the extensive travelling I did across states and villages during my army years. These outdoor experiences made me meet a variety of people, and from hearing about their favourite songs, I gradually and consciously learnt what makes a song popular.

'Yet another thing that has subconsciously helped me: my fears. The fear of being alone I began to feel after my Maaji departed. The fear of financial deprivation, I first encountered on the night of 2 October 1947 when we became refugees and broke overnight. And, many years later in the 1970s, even after I became very successful, the fear that I will not be able to deliver the next song and that it's all over now, and that I will soon be exposed as a fraud or fluke began to overwhelm me. Ironically, *yahi darr mujhe shakti bhi deta hai* (the same fear gives me strength) to do better. I wrote a poem to sing to myself whenever fear of failure overwhelms me, "*Main koi barf nahi hoon jo pighal jaaonga*". I gifted it to my dear friend Subhash Ghai decades later in February 2002. But my passion to write comes from my need to express my innermost feelings. I don't talk much otherwise, but there is so much I want to say, and songwriting is my way of doing that.

'My advice to youngsters: a song must have metre and rhythm. I whistle most of the time while writing my songs. Some tunes are given to me by the music director and some come to me naturally while writing. Further, I would advise youngsters to read a lot. Daily. Literature. Jokes. Read the poetry of the legends. Learn music if you want to be a lyricist. Learn Hindi and Urdu. The box office is unpredictable and has a *rangeen mizaaj* (colourful temperament), just like us writers. Unless you are a romantic and a highly sensitive mind, you cannot write. Most importantly, harbour *hausla* within yourself.

'I encouraged and worked with many new music directors when I became established, because *kabhi main bhi toh naya tha* (there was a time when I, too, was a novice). It is my way to pay back the encouragement I had received from established film-makers, composers and lyricists.

'S.D. Burman Dada spoke little Urdu or Hindi, and I learnt from him, right in the beginning of my career. He took great pains to understand the story and the lyrics before moulding the lyrics into a song. He reaffirmed my own belief in hearing the story keenly to do justice to a song.'

Here, I must share an incident about the time I fell in love with a girl during my college days and Dad found out about it. He told me to stop all this 'nonsense' immediately. I responded, 'But Dad, what about all those love songs you have written? It's you who said, "*Jab hum jawan honge*" in *Betaab*, "*Kya yahi pyar hai*" in *Rocky*, "*Dil kya kare, jab kisi ko, kisi se pyaar ho jaye*" in *Julie*, "*Main shayar toh nahin, magar ae haseen, jab se dekha, maine tujhko, shayari aa gayi*" in *Bobby*.'

He replied, 'I write these songs for characters in films. It's fiction. I have not written them to set an example for you to have an affair when it's your time and age to study!' So, you see, the lyricist in Dad drew a line between family life and work. In his defence, I would add that he did not complete high school, so he must have felt that since we had the privilege to go to college, we could have friends who were girls but not a 'girlfriend' at that stage of our life. That was what he must have intended to get across.

On His Romantic Songs

'I have not led a very romantic life, and that's why I am able to write romantic songs. Once you achieve something, you lose interest in it or the passion fades. Maybe because I am still aspiring for a romantic life, I can write aspirational romantic songs. Maybe my romantic compositions are the result of my repressed feelings, which I probably have deep within me but have never thought of seriously. Though my verses are sensitive and passionate, it has never occurred to me that they have an unseen romanticism attached to them. I have many unsaid, unspoken things inside me, and I guess I simply pen these down.

'I don't write all my songs from my own experiences. I wrote "Doli Ho Doli", for *Rajput*, before my daughters got married. After I wrote

"Chitthi Aayee Hai" for *Naam,* I sang the song at a wedding function in Delhi. The guests came up to me and asked which foreign land my children are settled in. Did I write this song missing them? I told them my children have always lived with me. There are many standard situations in life we all go through, and poets and authors have written of the emotions involved in these situations. I have read many of them, so I do not have to necessarily live these situations myself to write about them.'

In the song 'Doli Ho Doli', he writes, '*Doli ho doli, jab jab guzari, tu jiss dagar se, bichada koi humjoli.*' He compares the father–daughter relationship to a fond companionship, of *humjolis.* Nearly every time he sang this song at parties for family and friends, he would have tears in his eyes, and then it would become the last song for that night. The first time I saw my daddy cry was at the *doli* function of my sister Suman's wedding, just when she had got into the car and was being driven away. I was a teenager then.

The next time I saw him cry was nearly twenty-five years later, sometime in 2001, when he had become too weak because of the recurring bouts of asthma over many months and had lost most of his independence. Perhaps he saw this as a loss of dignity.

Writing in Folk and Lok-Geet Style

'Lok geet are folkish and so they are simple to understand. They make the listener feel *ek apnapan* (a sense of belonging). Most listeners can relate to the lyrics easily, so the song gets popular. The sweetest song is that which is sung for the common man. I get fan mail every day from common people from across India, complimenting me for the simplicity of my lyrics. Even my well-to-do friends and relatives say the same thing. My lack of higher formal education is the reason why I write using simple words. I have a very limited, school-level Hindi vocabulary. I write all my songs in the Urdu script. *Main seedhi baat likhata hoon, lekin maine gehari baat likhne ki koshish hamesha ki hai*

(I write simple things, but at the same time I always try to write things that have a deep meaning).

'Often, I have refused to write lyrics to a tune that did not appeal to me. Most music composers I have worked with would willingly make another one. That is a very good quality in a good composer. They do not feel hurt if a lyricist rejects their tunes. R.D. Burman would never mind creating a tune that appealed to me and helped me do a better job.

'Many talents, other than me, contribute to my song's success. The contribution of the music director, singer and songwriter to the success of a film and its songs is important, as the long-term value of a film is determined by the music. I have seen that when a film-maker or an actor passes away, their film's songs are played on TV and radio as a tribute, and not their film's scenes . . . The directors and scriptwriters, too, deserve credit for us lyricists churning out a good song. I must have worked with at least 250 directors so far, and the most with Rama Rao, Raj Khosla and Subhash Ghai. All three, as well as Yash Chopra, had a great sense of music. I find writing easy only when the story, situation and characters have been explained in depth to me. Maybe that's the reason why only talented directors get my best output—they help me visualize better.

'Certain film-makers have a very good ear for music, and so they select good tunes from the available options. They do deserve credit for their selection, and they inspire me to give my best. I have no patience for film-makers who do not know their job and yet interfere in my work.

'Every writer or person in any profession goes through three stages. First, striving for recognition and success. Second, attaining the success they worked so hard for. Third, either maintaining or losing that success. The third stage is the most difficult. In the first stage, you are most determined and focused and hungry! In the second stage, you realize your potential but also get a lot of attention, compliments, flattery; you get invited by everybody to their parties, functions. In the third stage, you have to avoid those second-stage distractions; you go to those parties but try not to get lost there and continue being as focused as you were during Stage One, when you were on your path to Stage Two. When a person becomes successful, he or she becomes more concerned about his health and personality, and forgets what brought him to that position or to the threshold of success. It's not easy to get success, but it's harder to keep it.

'Eighty per cent of the time, a suitable tune is created by the music director, and then I write the lyrics to suit the tune. Sometimes, the music director makes the tune after my lyrics are written. Often, I whistle my own suitable tune as I write. I wrote the song "Ishq Bina Kya Jeena Yaaron", for *Taal*, without having a tune.

'A song can be born in less than 15–20 minutes, or it can even take 5–6 days. In my profession, a writer cannot wait for inspiration to strike, as shooting schedules are fixed in advance. A poet writing a poetry book has the freedom to take months to write a page. Not the lyricist. I have to deliver the lyrics before the deadline. A lyricist must understand rhythm and have a flair for music. If the director has a good sense of music, my job only becomes easier, because he makes good choices without dilly-dallying. Once the beginning verse, the mukhda, arrives, I find it very easy to write the rest. Whether it takes fifteen minutes to write a song or five days, it does not reflect on the quality of the song; someone may finish bathing in ten minutes and come out cleaner than the one who takes thirty minutes. A film-maker can only inspire a lyricist by being receptive to good poetry, having knowledge of rhythm and being a sensitive person himself. Raj Kapoor liked "*Hum tum ek kamre mein bandh ho, aur chaabi kho jaye*" so much that he devised a situation in his film *Bobby* for it. Similarly, when Sanjay Khan heard me sing "*Maine poocha chand se, ke dekha hai kahin, mere yaar sa haseen*", he used it in *Abdullah*. Both the songs were not written for any film.

'I don't work according to "mood". I don't believe in mood. I believe I must do what I can do, when I can, and don't wait for a certain disposition and inspiration. *Mood aur mahol, likhne ka, dono khud dimaag mein banana padta hai, Yeh dimagi baatein hain, saara khel dimaag ka hai. Inspiration, yeh kya hota hai?* (Mood and atmosphere, it's all about the mind. It's a mind game. Inspiration? What's that?) When the work is important to you and it's important to the person paying you, the mind works automatically towards it; no great inspiration or particular time of day or mood is necessary then.'

All or Nothing

'It's better if a film has only one lyricist, because a film's songs must form a common thread running through the narrative. That is why I mostly insist that I must be the only lyricist in the films I write for. Producers, directors, even actors and music directors, were happy granting me that privilege.

'I think the reason my songs are popular could be that I consciously chose to write simply. I used words that some other popular lyricists were not using. I wrote from experience, always keeping in mind the story and characters, so that the song leaves an impression of the characters (expressing the lyrics in the film) on the listener's mind. Somehow, some beautiful lyrics happened to be born of this method, like *"Zindagi ke safar mein guzar jaate hain jo mukaam"* or *"Zikr hota hai jab qayamat ka, tere jalwon ki baat hoti hai"*. Moreover, I was lucky to have had the company of great music composers, singers, musicians, directors and writers who wrote the scripts that inspired the director and me.

'I do not go for walks or to the mountains to feel inspired. I have written most of my songs in my bedroom, and I complete them during music sittings with the director and composer. Often, I have written entire songs during the sittings. The film's story and my need to write songs are my inspiration. Producers spend crores on films; they cannot wait for us lyricists to get inspired.

'There is no secret behind what inspires me. Every human heart has emotions, gathered in the process of living. Unwittingly, they pour out into the verses. There is nothing more mysterious than unrequited love, and that's another great source of inspiration for me. Folk songs, too, inspire me. For the song "Main Jat Yamla Pagla Diwana" from *Pratiggya*, I was inspired by a Punjabi quote. For *"Maar diya jaye, ke chhod diya jaye"*, from *Mera Gaon Mera Desh*, I was inspired by the dialogue between King Porus and Alexander the Great, who had used almost the very same lines while wondering whether to spare King Porus's life or kill him: *"Tumhare saath kya salook kiya jaye?"*

'Producer-director Vijay Anand had once told me, "Bakshi Sa'ab, your songs take the story ahead, they play the role of the film's dialogues." "Maar Diya Jaye . . ." is one of many examples. During a song sitting for *Aan Milo Sajna*, Laxmikant–Pyarelal and I tried for many hours to get a breakthrough but failed. Tired, I got up to leave the sitting and remarked, *"Acha toh hum chalte hain."* Laxmikant asked me in response, *"Phir kab miloge?"* And thus I was inspired to make the mukhda of the song out of it. It was a big hit.

'I wrote about fifty verses for the *Betaab* song *"Jab hum jawan honge, jaane kahan honge"*. I usually create at least ten *antaras* for all my songs and then let the director choose three or four of what he or she finds most appropriate for their song situation and story. I gave Mahesh Bhatt fifteen antaras for the song in *Zakhm*, *"Tum aaye toh aaya mujhe yaad, gali mein aaj chand nikla."* He asked me why I wrote so many verses when he needed only three. But I believe, as a seller, I must give my buyer many options to help him make the right decision. I don't like a seller forcing his commodity on to a buyer and expecting the buyer to pay him too. People pay their hard-earned money for entertainment, so they deserve the best, from all departments of film-making, including lyrics, music.'

About Dad, Mahesh Bhatt once told me, 'Bakshi Sa'ab was a steady flame, with a sound mind. He wrote from the wisdom that emanated from a living reference point. No abstract thought. Surprisingly, he was not in awe of his own image. He emanated a raw wisdom that does not necessarily arise from reading books. He took inspiration from the story and nature. I asked him to write a song for *Zakhm*. He asked me about the characters: How often does the man of the house visit his family, the woman he loves and has a child with but does not marry? I told him that the father comes home once in a blue moon only to see his family. Within seconds, Bakshiji wrote, "*Tum aaye toh aaya mujhe yaad, gali mein aaj chand nikla.*" He equated the blue moon with *Eid ka chand, jo ki kabhi kabhi nikalta hai.*'

Versatility

'I don't get attached to any one particular music director. I work with everyone who I feel can do justice to the film's needs, and that allows me quantity, versatility and quality as a songwriter. Interacting with such a variety of creative people keeps me in touch with the whole spectrum of film music and its listeners.

He worked with music composers across generations, with fathers as well as sons: S.D. Burman and R.D. Burman, Roshan and Rajesh Roshan, Kalyanji–Anandji and Viju Shah (son of Kalyanji), Chitragupt and Anand–Milind, Nadeem–Shravan and Sanjeev–Darshan (sons of Shravan Rathod), Anil Biswas and his sons Amar–Utpal.

'I get along with most music directors because I do not have an ego about what I write. And since I write most songs quickly, they are happy working with me. I have never asked any producer to take me to a hill station, abroad or to a riverside lodge to write their songs, which saves them money. So they like working with me.'

Change of Style

'If the tune is catchy, listeners tend to overlook the words. I got away using many Punjabi words, and even whole verses, in my Hindi lyrics because of this. "Bindiya Chamkegi" is one example. The song was a very big hit. I have since written many songs that have Punjabi verses slipped into them. D.N. Madhok, who was born in Gujranwala, was one of the first Punjabis to write film songs. He was the first lyricist to introduce Punjabi in Hindi film songs. Geet and nazm are related; a geet is simply poetry that can be expressed in melody. Being conversant with Urdu/Hindi and *saral* Hindustani, Punjabis were able to write geets easily, like Sahir. Even Shailendra was born in Rawalpindi. We Punjabis brought our *tappas* and *kafias* into our *filmy* geets.

'In a way, not just *Jab Jab Phool Khile* (1965) but also *Farz* (1967) was a turning point for me, in terms of writing lyrics in a conversational manner. After that, I wrote my songs in a lighter vein, in everyday, conversational Hindustani. The songs and film were very big hits, which encouraged me to continue in that style.'

The birthday song from *Farz*, 'Baar Baar Din Ye Aaye', remains popular even today.

Whenever Dad received travel conveyance allowance for attending his song recordings, he would hand it over to our driver or some musician he knew was in need of financial assistance. Sometime in the late '70s, I asked him why he did not pocket the petrol allowance paid to him for recordings. 'I need their blessings too, not just my talent and hard work, to get work and find success. If they earn something from every recording of mine, beyond the salary I pay our driver or the fees someone earns as a musician, they must be praying to their God daily, asking that I be blessed with a song recording. *Sab ko saath mein lekar chalna padhta hai* (One has to take everyone along). Maybe my luck is good because of their prayers, and it's not just God's blessing.'

Poet or Lyricist?

'It's more difficult to write film lyrics than poetry. You have to write within boundaries. Songwriting has limitations imposed by time, thought and the characters the song is written for. Although we differentiate between the two categories, a lyricist is a poet too . . .

'There are certain peculiar qualifications you have to fulfil to be called a poet. You need to take part in mushairas and contribute to Hindi or Urdu literature. And our lyrics writers don't get recognition as poets and are not seen to be contributing to literature.

'Unlike poetry, film songs are written for films that cost lakhs of rupees to make. So, the song must get popular, to help the film earn repeat value and thus recover its cost of production. It's a challenge to write film songs.

'A poet arrives alone, but a lyricist comes with an orchestra. The main difference between a poet and a songwriter is that a poet remains immersed in his mood, his temperament, and writes to satisfy his own creative urge, whereas in songwriting, in the very same film, you may have to write a love song, a prayer, a cabaret dance, a background score that takes the story forward. The biggest challenge is to write a song that takes the narrative forward, within the bounds of characterization, time limit and storyline. *Hazaron rang milke, ek rang banta hai* (Thousands of hues come together to form a single colour). You have to think on the spot, fast, with the director, music director, musicians all looking at you with their expectations and at their watches. A good songwriter has to be a good craftsman, more than a good poet. For me, rhyming is very important. But a lyricist has to come to the point at once. Unlike a poet, he does not have the space and time to beat around the bush. In a song in *Aaye Din Bahar Ke*, the hero directs his anger towards his unfaithful lover directly in the mukhda, "*Mere dushman tu meri dosti ko tarse,*" and the poetic expression of thought lies in the antara, "*Tu phool bane patjhad ka, tujhpe bahaar na aye kabhi.*"'

Writing for Love

'I love writing for pairs—Dilip Kumar and Saira, Shashi Kapoor and Nanda, Rajesh Khanna and Mumtaz, Rishi Kapoor and Dimple, Kumar Gaurav and Vijayta, Sunny Deol and Poonam Dhillon, Dev Anand and Zeenat Aman, Sunny Deol and Amrita, Rajesh Khanna and Sharmila Tagore, Dharmendra and Hema, Amitabh Bachchan and Parveen Babi, Kamal Haasan and Rati Agnihotri, Fardeen and Amrita Arora, Hrithik and Kareena and Esha Deol, Sanjay Dutt and Tina Munim, Anil Kapoor and Padmini, among many other *jodis* . . . I think I have written songs for nearly seventy films starring Dharmendra, sixty-two starring Jeetendra, forty-five starring Rajesh Khanna, forty-four starring Amitabh Bachchan, forty-two starring Hema Malini, thirty-six starring Rekha, twenty-six starring Mumtaz, twenty-three starring Madhuri Dixit and twenty-one starring Sridevi.

'I believe in destiny. Let me give you an example. S.D. Burman Dada introduced me to the great director Guru Dutt, to write lyrics for *Kaagaz Ke Phool*. But Guru Dutt preferred to work with Kaifi Azmi Sa'ab. I considered myself unlucky, unfortunate, that I did not get to write for that film. I cursed my luck for a year. The film released, and it bombed at the box office. I felt God had saved me, destiny had saved me. I already had a flop behind me, *Bhala Admi*, and if I had been the writer for *Kaagaz Ke Phool*, I would have had a second flop to my name, and my career would have been over before even beginning. In this industry, they worship the rising sun. They don't worship you; they worship your hits, not your talent.

'Whenever I wrote for Rajesh Khanna, I kept in mind the voice of Kishore Kumar and intentionally wrote smooth-flowing lyrics for him. Some people say I gave Rajesh Khanna hit songs, and even Kaka (Rajesh Khanna) says I made his life by giving him great songs. But I believe Rajesh Khanna made our songs hits by singing (or lip-syncing to) them. Let us not forget, the actor is the face of our songs. We lyricists are best if invisible. The audience must feel it's the character's song, not mine, not R.D. Burman's, etc.'

Success and Failure

'Success should not make you complacent. If you have won one race, there is no guarantee you will win the next. You may have to try harder for the next race. In my songs, I have never tried to project myself at the expense of a film's story. The story is more important than my success as a lyricist or my "style" of writing. If the audience recognizes my words in a song, then I feel I have failed, even if the song is a hit. My words are supposed to originate from and belong to the characters in that story, that film, and not to me, the lyricist. I once suggested that my song be dropped from the film *Milan*, a day after the premiere, as my words did not gel with the character singing. This song was, "*Aaj dil pe koi, zor chalta nahin, muskurane lage the, magar ro padhe.*" I wrote it as poetry, without keeping in mind the character. When I saw it on the screen, I could not believe that the character in that film could sing these "literary" verses. The film-makers agreed with my suggestion and dropped it.

Another time he felt he did not do a good job at lyrics writing was after he watched the film *Andha Kanoon* and saw the protagonist singing the song "*Rote rote hasna seekho, haste haste, rona, jitni chabi bhari Ram ne, utna chale khilona*". The protagonist is not a Hindu and uses the name of a Hindu God. Dad told us, 'I made a mistake in not asking the director the name and religion of the character I was writing this song for. The director, while narrating the story and situation to me, kept referring to the lead character by the actor's name, Mr Bachchan. Had I known Amitabh Bachchan was playing a Muslim character in the film, I would have used an example more suitable to the character's belief and culture.'

It should be said that a Muslim protagonist taking a Hindu God's name in a song, or vice versa, is nothing out of the ordinary in Indian culture and films. It is an example of the inherent secularism of our culture. The reason the lyricist thought of this as a failure on his part was because he would have written in such a way only if the director had instructed him to flesh out the protagonist's secular nature subtly in the lyrics. He was a lyricist who stuck to the client's brief.

Age Is Just a Number

'Age does not matter when it comes to writing love songs. I wrote for *Bobby* at forty-four, *Ek Duje Ke Liye* at fifty-two, *Saudagar* at sixty-one, *Dilwale Dulhania Le Jayenge* and *Dil Toh Pagal Hai* in my 60s. Likewise for philosophical songs. I wrote "*Zindagi ke safar mein guzar jate hain jo mukaam*", for *Aap Ki Kasam*, in my 30s . . . Age has not been factor in my association with composers. I was below thirty when I worked, successfully, with Roshan, S.D. Burman Dada. The only disadvantage is that now, when I work with young composers like Viju Shah, Anand–Milind or the children of film-makers whom I have known for a long time, they hesitate to find fault with my lyrics. That makes my work suffer. After all, I need healthy criticism to write appropriately. So, it's the situation, a story, a character, a tune that inspires me to write. Not my age.'

Times Have Changed

'We do not need a censor board to reject vulgar lyrics. The audience will do that job. The controversy over my song "Choli Ke Peeche Kya Hai" (*Khal Nayak*) pained me, as I'd simply written it in an allusive style. I prefer allusion to literal words, as literal words tend to sound vulgar, and I take inspiration from our folk songs, which are full of such imagery and allusions. My children are my barometer. I write keeping in mind that my children may end up singing these songs.

He was once asked about his views on the flak he had received for writing 'Choli Ke Peeche Kya Hai'. He smiled and said instantly, without annoyance or bitterness, 'Those who are accusing me of writing double-meaning lyrics, their *nazar* (eyes) and *dhyan* (focus) are on her choli, not on my lyrics.'

'Times have changed; our films have changed, and so our songs will change too. Today, our onscreen pairs declare their love for each other too quickly, without justification. The same goes for the other emotions—anger, hatred, jealousy, dejection, rejection, fulfilment. Today, most films progress at a fast pace, and directors have less scope to build up emotions, so naturally, our songs too have become fast-paced to suit the fast-paced scenes. Since the music has fast beats, we compose quick, short lines to accompany them. There was a time when film-makers like Bimal Roy could express "I love you" without the characters having to say the words at all. Many of today's film-makers are ignorant of these subtle nuances . . .

'There is an economic and commercial reason behind film-making and thus, the lyricist has to deliver a song quickly and make changes during the recording as someone's money is on the line. You make money when they make money . . .

'It's been years since I wrote a sad song. I miss writing sad songs. There are very few sad songs in our films nowadays. Does this mean people are so happy nowadays that sad situations don't reflect in our stories any more? Or does it mean that there is so much sadness in life that we neither want to see it on screen nor hear it in songs?'

A Superstitious Industry

Sometime in the late '80s, I happened to begin wearing short pants and half-sleeved T-shirts for song recordings. The films did well. There were many music directors and film-makers at that time who would send me back if I ever turned up in full pants at their recordings and ask me to return in my lucky shorts. This is a very superstitious industry. Every film I sang in was a box-office flop, and so, the industry being superstitious, they stopped asking me to sing in their films. I stopped singing after *Sholay*. The film was a blockbuster, but the qawwali I sang in it was not part of the final cut. People will certainly remember me for my hit lyrics, but I also wish to be remembered for at least one of the songs I sang.

'I was thrilled when Raj Kapoor wanted me to write the songs for his son Rishi Kapoor's launch film. He invited Laxmikant–Pyarelal and me to his studio for a song sitting. I had not heard the story but knew the film was titled *Bobby*. When we met Raj Kapoor, I told him I have written a verse and recited it to him: *"Hum tum, ek kamre mein bandh hon, aur chabi kho jaye; tere naino ki bhool bhulaiya mein, Bobby kho jaye."* I asked him if Bobby was the name of the hero or heroine and if we could use this line for a song in the film. He liked the verse and said that the line would be a good fit for either of the genders. He also told me that though there was no such situation in the story, which we were yet to hear, he would create one for this song. I got the idea for this song from my first visit to Laxmikant's new bungalow in Juhu; there were so many rooms that I got lost on my first visit there.

'Inspiration can strike at any moment. Once, Shakti Samantha, R.D. Burman and I were at a film party at the Sun-n-Sand hotel in Juhu. After we were done, we were waiting for our cars to arrive and it was pouring heavily. I lit my cigarette and threw the burning match out in the pouring rain to extinguish it. That's when I thought of the verse, *"Chingari koi bhadke, toh saawan usse bujhaye, saawan jo, agan lagaye, usse kaun bujhaye . . ."* Shakti Da liked it and created a situation in the film, *Amar Prem*, so that the line could be used as the mukhda of the song I later wrote.'

'*Meri ek hi kamzori hai ki mere geet jan bhasha mein hote hain* (My only weakness is that my songs are in the language of the common people).' I am always surprised when I read that statement by my father. Some critics and lyricists accused him of being a non-writer, a non-poet, and that hurt him. Perhaps that was why he even ended up writing, by his own admission, songs in his 'defence', songs like 'Main Shayar Toh Nahi' and 'Main Shayar Badnaam'. What his listeners and many journalists have time and again termed as his strength, he saw as his weakness.

'Why do some really good lyricists say they are "forced" to write film songs to run their homes? Why do people look down on film songs? Should a film lyricist not look at his work as something to be proud of? I write simple because I am not highly educated, but I also know by writing simple lyrics I can appeal to many people across India who are not highly educated and love my songs.

'I have knowingly and unknowingly learnt a lot from senior writers, so I respect them all, always. I am able to write and express new thoughts in my songs because I read a lot daily. One who does not read will have nothing new to talk about. I love Urdu literature, and my favourite magazine is the *Reader's Digest*.

'I wrote the song *"Mere jeevan saathi, pyar kiye jaa"*, for *Ek Duje Ke Liye*, using only Hindi film titles, nearly 200–250, with the help of my composers Laxmikant–Pyarelal. The character (played by Kamal Haasan) cannot speak Hindi, and the heroine (played by Rati) tells him, "If you love me, you must learn to speak Hindi." So to impress her, he sings a song for her using popular Hindi film names. Every word in this song is a film title. This situational song takes their friendship ahead towards a romance, and thus it takes their love story ahead. About *Ek Duje Ke Liye* and the contribution a film's songs can make to its success, the lyricist Hasrat Jaipuri Sa'ab said, "If you remove the songs from *Ek Duje Ke Liye*, the film will crash." I don't agree with him, but I understand that he was making the case for us lyricists. Hasrat Sa'ab, I think, was the king of romance.'

Working Process

'Before beginning a song, I would always ask which actors were going to lip-sync to the song and write according to that. For Rajesh Khanna's songs, I would keep in mind Kishore Kumar's voice and write . . .'

'*Maine kabhi hit gaana nahi likha; gaana public hit ya flop karti hai* (It's not me who writes a hit song; it's the public that determines whether a song becomes a hit or a flop). When producers or directors ask me to write them a hit song, I tell them they have come to the wrong person. This shop does not sell hits. *Iss dukaan pe hit gaane nahi milte.*

'Army life and the work of a lyricist are similar. Both require good conduct to work in harmony like a team, and in both these fields you need recommendations from your seniors and peers.'

'I learnt early on that you cannot force your language skills on listeners; they reject what they can't comprehend by not singing it. A song becomes popular if you can sing it easily.'

'I cannot recollect my own songs even immediately after writing them. Perhaps my mind, on its own, wipes the slate clean to be able to write the next one.'

'*Main samaaj ko jodne waale geet likhta hoon, todne waale nahi* (I write songs that bring people together not drive them apart).' One example being, '*Mere desh premiyon, aapas mein prem karo, desh premiyon*', from *Desh Premee*.

Race for Awards

'Once, I was approached by a person who promised me that year's major film award, if I gave him Rs 11,000. This was sometime in the '70s. My songs were doing very well, I was on the top, but I was not winning awards. I said to him, "You say that if I pay you the sum of Rs 11,000, you can guarantee me an award. But will your award guarantee me work?" He replied, "No, I can only guarantee the award." I told him that I'd rather just work to get more work.

Sometime in the '90s, I asked Dad why he had received so many nominations but won only a few awards. I told him if he could arrange for some PR representative for himself, he might win more awards. This is what he said:

'Destiny is all-powerful. I don't believe in manipulations for work or awards. It's certainly encouraging to receive awards, but I don't crave for them anymore. The awards that I have won, I have to leave them behind; they can decorate our living room long after I am gone. The award that will travel with me to my next birth I won way back in the '70s/'80s. I received a letter from a stranger residing in a village. He wrote that he had decided to commit suicide, had even gone and lain on the railway tracks passing through his village. But just then, a song reached his ears. A radio, perhaps, was playing nearby, and the wind must have carried the song along. The verse that happened to reach his ears as he waited for the train to arrive, was, "*Gaadi ka naam, na kar badnaam, patri pe rakh ke sar ko; himmat na haar, kar intezaar, aa laut jayein ghar ko; yeh raat jaa rahi hai, woh subah aa rahi hai.*" The man got up from the tracks, and just then the train hurtled past him. He wrote to tell me that my lyrics had saved his life. That is the biggest award I have won. *Duniya mein aisa koi kaam nahi, jiss mein har saal bonus milna hi chahiye, ya phir milta hi hai.*

'Writing good lyrics is important, but they may not necessarily become popular or win awards. In *Ek Duje Ke Liye*, I preferred "*Solah baras ki, bali umar ko salaam, pyar teri pehli nazar ko salaam*" as a song, for its lyrics. But it was not even nominated. Instead, I was awarded for "*Tere mere beech mein, kaisa hai yeh bandhan anjaana, maine nahi jaana, tune nahi jaana*', from the same film. The same happened with *Dilwale Dulhania Le Jayenge*—I was awarded for "Tujhe Dekha Toh Yeh Jaana Sanam" but I preferred "Ghar Aaja Pardesi". However, I was not upset, because in some awards, popularity matters to the judges more than the quality. Moreover, it is not enough that a song should become a hit and win awards. A song that deserves an award should also be the one that moves the story ahead. Further, a correct song situation and proper picturization help make a memorable song, instead of just a successful one . . .

'Just as any other creative person in film-making, I too am vulnerable, because the success of our songs also depends on how the others have co-presented it—the director, music director, choreographer, cinematographer. It's teamwork. So, if a song does not get an award, every one of us has to work harder to rise to the challenges posed by various unpredictable factors in this business. Film-making, songs are all about teamwork, *aur humme ek orchestra ki tarhan saath chalne ki himmat aur kabliyat honi chahiye* (and we need to pull together with the courage and skill of an orchestra).'

Sometime in February 2002, Dad dictated this letter to me:

My song from *Gadar: Ek Prem Katha*, 'Udja Kale Kawan', did not get an award. Many years ago, the singer Mukesh and I cried when our song from *Milan* did not get any of the awards that we both felt it deserved; 'Saawan Ka Mahina' was a popular and appreciated song of that year, along with the popular and deserving 'Mere Desh Ki Dharti'. Post our tears, we both kept quiet about the choices that had been made, on behalf of millions, by a select few in positions of 'power'. How fair that is, is open to question and will always be. I remained silent over the next few decades, receiving forty Filmfare Award nominations and eventually four awards . . . Thank you, Filmfare and the people who made the choice for Filmfare . . .

I did not do this earlier, so I want to do it now, even though winning awards in the past made me feel happy and motivated me to go on doing even better work for my listeners. Yet I hereby want to formally withdraw from this 'competition', or rather this 'race', for awards. Moreover, I did not come here to become an award winner. I came here because I loved writing film songs—it was a childhood dream—and because I needed money for the security of my family, particularly after the partition of India, as we were literally homeless and not well-off financially.

I request that my name not be included in the nominations for any award hereafter. I have worked with star composers, from Naushad and S.D. Burman to A.R. Rahman. I am happy; that is a big award too.

My biggest reward is that my dream was eventually fulfilled, thanks to time and God, and also that I was able to secure my family financially and that so many people love my songs. My family and relatives, close friends and colleagues, as well as eminent people like Subhash Ghai, Javed Akhtar and Sameer constantly compliment me for my work. These are the rewards that awards cannot earn someone.

After writing more than a thousand good and popular/hit songs, out of the 3500–4000 I have written, I do not now want to sit in this annual 'examination' called AWARDS. I particularly lost faith in them when 'Sawan Ka Mahina' did not win one. Back then, I had thought, 'If such a good song cannot earn me an award, I think I will never be able to write anything better than this song in my lifetime. So I should not expect an award hereafter.' I, and many others in this world, should not sit in the examination halls year after year for their work which earns them rewards that awards cannot ever match. The awards people will give me, or have given me, I will leave them behind to decorate my house. The reward that awards cannot bring me—like my song that happened to save ONE HUMAN LIFE—my soul will carry when it leaves the cage of this body, which I feel is now getting sick and will not last.

I don't want to die so soon, only because I have hundreds of more unsaid feelings and songs in me. I am not sad that I will die; I am sad that I cannot give those unwritten and unsung songs to anyone, not even to my beloved children, before I go away, because what came with me has to leave with me. No one can gift such things to anyone as an inheritance or out of generosity or foolishness.

In the past, whenever I got an award for my song, I went to the stage and accepted it with thanks and never spoke more than two or three words. Many people would tell me, 'You should have also spoken something about the award, the song, about your life.' I would always reply to them, 'But I do not find any reason to talk. Let my work speak.' Anyway, I received a lot of love from my family, friends and millions of listeners. And I have received very few awards to be able to tell someone, 'Hey, listen, I am an award winner too.'

Now, the time has come. I am sick, and I should speak the truth. I do not want to go on having discussions about awards, etc., which will never end nor reach any conclusion. Let the listeners judge who is award-worthy and who reward-worthy. I just request you, the readers of this letter, and the 'awards *waale log*' to kindly excuse me and delete my name from your future competitions, from your race to nowhere. I have somewhere to reach, somewhere to go. So, I hereby withdraw my name from the whole 'commercial *sangram* (struggle) of awards'. Even a very popular poet, the only poet-cum-lyricist I had known, who helped me a lot when I was a NOBODY, had said the same thing about the 'commercial sangram of awards'. Respect to all. Thank you very much. *Acha, toh hum ab chalte hain.*

Your Own Voice, Your Own Story

Once, Sidharth, a friend of mine, came over to our place, because he wanted Dad to hear him sing and offer him guidance on his singing. He told Dad that he sings like Mohammed Rafi. Dad said to my aspiring singer pal that he was no longer interested in hearing him sing, that if he wanted to hear Rafi, we had many CDs and vinyls of his songs. Why would he want to hear a copycat? He advised my friend, 'Go find your own voice. Only then I would be interested to hear you and can offer you guidance. You need to have your own unique voice to stand apart from the others.'

'When Aditya Chopra narrated to me the story of *Dilwale Dulhania Le Jayenge*, I told him, "Adi, even if you make 50 per cent of what you just narrated to me, your film will be a big hit." After the premiere, I called Adi and said, "You have made 100 per cent of what you had narrated to me. Your film is going to be a very big hit." The film ran for years.'

It is understandable that he was a good judge of stories. By the mid-'90s, he had written songs for at least 500 films, and had maybe rejected at least 200–500 films after hearing the stories. When you have heard the narratives of so many films, it can make your sense of story sharp.

'There was a seemingly unstable guest living next door when I was staying at a guest house in Khar West. He would sit in the veranda and have his breakfast. When I would pass by, on my way to look for work, and wish him, he would respond by picking up his small packet of butter and pretending to throw it at me. He probably disliked me because I spent all my time reading and writing, and never indulged him. It was scary as I felt that one day, he was going to whack me with the butter. Then, one day, he actually threw it at me and missed. Scared, I decided to change my room. However, the lesson I took from it was, *makhan se maaro, ya patthar se, lekin nishaana lagna chahiye* (whether it's butter or a stone you're throwing at someone, make sure you hit the target). Whatever be your choice of words, a lyricist must be able to convey the story of the moment in the screenplay. You must have a good aim and never miss your target. I always write according to the story and have rarely missed my target.'

Respect and Disagreements

'Respect. That is what most people need. Even if they eat a smaller meal, they want a plate full of respect. A traffic hawaldar once stopped me for breaking the red light. I got off my car, walked up to him, stopped at a respectful distance and gave him my military-style salute. He laughed and saluted back, and he told me to buzz off and not to break a light again. He had not let me off because he recognized my face. I have *always* shown similar respect to the producers who pay me for the job they expect me to perform to the best of my abilities. I have never treated them like people who might pay me less or ask for too much while paying too little.

'There are good ways to show producers and directors that you disagree with them, without insulting them or shouting at them. Once my chauffer was overspeeding at Worli Sea Face, in spite of repeated reminders not to do so. This time, I told him to stop the car on the side of the road, and I got off. I hailed a taxi and asked him to reach home without me. He quietly followed us, and thereafter he never oversped. Once, B.R. Chopra Sa'ab and I were working on a film, and I was just not comprehending the story. It was my limitation, not his, but I did not want him to do this film with me. We had done good work together earlier in *Pati Patni Aur Woh*. I simply told him to excuse me from this project, but on one condition: that our friendship will continue and he won't stop inviting me to his house for meals, as they make the best non-vegetarian food I've ever had. Chopra Sa'ab laughed in pleasure and though we did not work together, he and his son, film-maker Ravi, continue to be my friends.

'Don't go ahead with what goes against your beliefs. Even if you have spent time and money on it. For instance, I am scared of heights and cannot take flights. I have returned many times from the airport without taking the flight; I did that because I felt I should not get on board, even after having purchased a ticket, and because my mind was full of fear. A panic attack in the air will be far costlier for everyone than a plane ticket is for me. Think of others.

'I met so many different people and wrote for so many different characters and stories over the years that it made me a better writer and person. I learnt from every song. In the same way, I learnt to be a father with every child. After all, I was not born as one.'

* * *

None of what he has said is gospel truth for the film industry and his profession. These statements just give us a sense of the way he thought and worked, of his perceptions and beliefs. From all that has been said, what stands out for me at the end of this chapter is how focused and pragmatic he was. To reiterate his words, 'I began writing first as a hobby, subsequently for the financial security of my family and continue because I cannot live without it. Some songs I wrote to run my kitchen, some for my heart. Doing my best for my music composers, film-makers and my family is my param kartavya. Moreover, I think my songwriting experiences have also made me a better person.'

9

'Mushkil Mein Hai Kaun Kisi Ka'

'I have never met a person who has given me more trouble than myself.' Dad would say this when he was trying to break free of his habits of chewing paan and smoking cigarettes. When he suffered his second heart attack, sometime in the '80s, and a pacemaker was implanted in his chest, his doctor advised him, 'Mr Bakshi, you must stop the bad habits you have cultivated for the last thirty years, of chewing paan and smoking. They have harmed your heart.'

After the doctor left, Dad remarked, 'This doctor knows nothing. It's not paan and tobacco that have harmed my heart. My songs have taken a toll on my heart.'

* * *

A Dichotomy

Though Dad suffered from self-doubt and a lack of confidence before embarking on a song, when he was challenged in any way about his 'worth' as a writer or human being, he knew how to give it back. Two incidents stand out for me, reflecting on the dichotomy of human nature.

The first one concerns our second home, our family house in Bhilar, in the hills of Panchgani, about five hours' drive from Mumbai.

Dad and Mom had built it together over a period of five years, and we would visit it only during our annual summer holidays. It had all the basic necessities and lacked any features that might be considered 'luxurious'—things expected in the house of a public figure like Anand Bakshi. A Pune-based industrialist had his opulent summer house in our neighbourhood. Sometimes, he would visit our home, or we would drop by to his place to see him. On one of his visits to our house, he told Dad, 'Mr Bakshi, I am surprised, rather quite shocked, at the way you live here! You should at least put granite on the floors and spend some more money on the interiors. It's in fashion. Build a cement roof; your tiled roof looks old-fashioned. You should hire an interior designer, and I can recommend the designer who decorated my house. A man like you deserves a better-looking house!'

After pondering a little over his unsolicited advice, Dad told him, 'I'm happy that your house is better looking than my simple home. For the past many years, when I come to this house, when I sit here on this simple veranda under my simple tiled roof, to enjoy the same sunshine that shines on your house too, I have been noticing one thing: People who happen to pass by the road in front of the house sometimes stop to point at me or the house and say, "This is Anand Bakshi's house." They look at my house with admiration. And you are feeling bad for me?!'

The other incident happened during a party hosted by an income tax officer. He requested Dad to sing. 'Bakshiji, I have heard that you sing very well. Sing for us some of your favourite songs tonight.'

My father replied, 'I love to sing, even though I don't sing well. But today, I am not feeling well. I have come here to this gathering just to pay my respects to my friend, the host. I will not be able to sing today. But I will definitely sing some other night, when we meet again someday, at our friend's house.'

The income tax officer replied, 'Mr Anand Bakshi, this is a party by income tax officers, for income tax officers, and I am an income tax officer telling you to sing for us. So consider this as an order and not just a request from a fan!'

Anand Bakshi took a leisurely sip of his drink and a deep puff of his 555. He looked at the arrogant officer and asked him, 'Sir, please tell me, what is your rank in the Income Tax department?'

The officer haughtily replied, 'Assistant commissioner of income tax!'

Bakshi took another sip of his drink and said, 'There must be 10,000, more or less, assistant commissioners of income tax in this city alone. There must be thousands of more across India. My dear assistant commissioner of income tax, people tell me there is only one Anand Bakshi in this country. When you reach a rank where you are the only one of your kind in your profession, you can order me to sing, and I will gladly sing for you alone if need be. But first, reach that rank in your own profession!' The officer did not cross my dad's path again the entire night.

* * *

'Main koi barf nahi hoon jo pighal jaoonga'

Now that you have travelled so far with me, let me introduce you to a very special self-expression of my father, *'Main koi barf nahi hoon jo pighal jaoonga.'* In the '90s, he began to be overwhelmed by anxiety, which he had been suffering from since the early '70s. He wouldn't, for instance, want to be home alone. He would always travel with a companion when he left the city for work or on a family vacation. He lacked confidence in his writing abilities. In spite of his success, he continued to feel like he wasn't good enough. So, he wrote a second poem to inspire himself, to boost his hausla. He wrote nearly 3300 songs for films, for others. This one he wrote for himself. But in the last year of his life, he gifted the poem to his dear friend and film-maker Subhash Ghai:

> *Main koi barf nahi hoon jo pighal jaoonga*
> *Main koi harf nahi hoon jo badal jaoonga.*
> *Main saharon pe nahi, khud pe yakin rakhta hoon*
> *Gir padunga toh huva kya, main sambhal jaoonga.*

Chand suraj ki tarah waqt pe nikla hoon main
Chand suraj ki tarah waqt pe dhal jaoonga.
Kaafile wale mujhe chhod gaye hain peeche
Kaafile walon se aage main nikal jaoonga.
Main andheron ko mita doonga, chiragon ki tarah
Aag seene mein laaga dunga, main jal jaoonga.
Husn walon se guzarish hai ki parda kar lein
Main dewaana hoon, main ashiq hoon, machal jaoonga.
Rok sakti hai mujhe toh rok le duniya, 'Bakhshi'
Main toh jaadu hoon, jaadu hoon chala jaoonga.

Sometime in the mid-'90s, as a cure for his nearly three decades of anxiety of being alone and lack of confidence as a lyricist, Anand Bakshi was advised by his family doctor to do the things he would do when he first arrived in Bombay as a 'struggler' looking for work. The doctor was of the opinion that if Bakshi relived his early years, of the '50s and '60s, when he was all alone, he would be able to regain his lost confidence. And so, as I have mentioned previously, Bakshi began travelling alone in Bombay's local trains, like he used to do in his days of struggle. He purchased a first-class Western Railway local train pass and would take the train from the Khar station to Marine Lines in the afternoons at least once a week; he did this for several months.

These are some of the notes he made in his personal diary in regard to those journeys:

Today I stood by the Sea Face at the Marine Drive promenade and prayed to the god of the seas, and acknowledged to the sea that I am just a drop unlike Him who is the seven seas. With help from God, I want to be free of my phobias before the end of this life. (6 December 1995)

Today I walked from the Dadar station to Bhagwan Dada's old office, where I had started my film life, earned my first break in films,

Bhala Admi. Then I disembarked at Mahim and walked to producer Hiren Khera's old office, where I had earned my first successful film, *Mehendi Lagi Mere Haath*, in which all songs were written by me. After reliving these emotional memories of my past, I think my phobias are dying. I should have made these journeys earlier, but I cannot fight destiny. I was destined to suffer all this while. The only person who has given me the most trouble is myself. (31 January 1996)

* * *

God and Faith

When you are alone you are with your God. That's God for me. That's the time I talk with my God. God is truth. This is the truth. And this life is nothing but a stage. We all are actors. For us, we are the audiences. We can see our own act play out. For others, we are actors. We have to appear in our acts on this stage and then disappear. Kings, queens, the richest, bravest, strongest, kindest persons came and went way. So will I. They could not change this act in the stage called world to suit themselves. Nor can I. So enjoy both the acts—happy and sad acts, good health and bad. (21 July 2001)

There is this fable Dad narrated to us on our regular family time together before dinner while he sipped a few pegs of his favourite Red Label on the balcony of our home when we were quite young.

Many centuries ago, at an important corner of several intersecting roads, stood tall a mandir, a gurdwara, a church, a fire temple, a masjid, a synagogue and all the other places of worship. At this significant crossroads, thousands of people were burning homes, looting and killing, out of hatred for the other's religion. Men, women, children and animals of the 'enemies' were not spared. The earth had turned red. People waded through the flowing blood of all races and creeds.

The tall minarets of the places of worship were watching the bloodbath silently. After a long while, one of the minarets remarks to the others, 'How about one of us gets off our high and mighty pedestal, go down to their level of existence and consciousness, and reveal to these fools the supreme truth: that we all are ONE! That there is no difference, between us, Gods. Go and inform them that their religions are different, their paths leading to us are different, but they all lead to us, and that we are not separate but ONE. I am confident this revelation will stop the bloodbath among our followers that we have all been witnessing silently for centuries. They are such idiots! They believe one of us is superior to the others. Some of them even believe that only they are the pure ones, the only "believers", while all others are non-believers!'

All the minarets giggle and snicker. They agree with this ultimate truth wisely spoken by one of them. But they continue to watch the bloodbath in silence.

Then, one of the minarets proceeds to shout at the crowd, ordering them to stop killing each other for their gods. However, all the other minarets immediately ask this 'outspoken' minaret to stop. They all protest together: 'You fool! Don't tell these great fools the truth, which only we all have always known. Or which some humans knew but were killed by the others. Let these fools fight. Because the day they realize we all are one, that we are all really ONE, they won't need us any longer, and that will be the day they will destroy us. Now they bow to us out of their ignorance and fear. Who else in this universe ever gave us so much importance? We have stood tall and have been superior to them for centuries only because of their fears and ignorance. If they learn the truth, that we are all ONE, they will not need us any more. Let us not lose the importance and superiority that we have enjoyed at their cost for centuries! Prior to that, nature had been more important than us! These very fools gave us birth and even made us immortal and raised us above them to the skies. Let us maintain status quo for our benefit.'

All of them ponder solemnly the consequences of revealing the truth to these stupid humans. They shake hands to remain silent forever, lest they be razed to the ground by 'intelligent humans'. Thus, the battle raged on, has raged on for centuries.

* * *

Integrity and Self-Worth

Another story narrated to us children: A film unit was shooting in a remote region of Punjab. One of the scenes required a doli (a bride's palanquin). The unit searched the whole village but could not find one. After looking a little further, they found one in a nearby village. They rushed to the location and met the woman who owned it; she was an old widow. She agreed to lend them the doli, and asked who the bride was and in which village the wedding was to take place. The film unit told her that there was no real bride, as it was going to be a fake wedding, with fake bride and groom, for a film shoot. The old lady, who lived off the income she earned lending dolis for weddings, refused to lend it to the film unit for a 'fake' bride. They offered her ten times the fee she had quoted. But the woman refused the offer, saying proudly, 'Sorry, only real brides are worthy of a doli.'

My father later told me, 'That's what I consider integrity and character. Don't get misled by money being offered in exchange for your values. You don't have to conform to the world around you. Be unique.'

* * *

'You don't have to conform to the world around you'

When Dad went to purchase his first car, a second-hand Fiat, 1964 model, the seller agreed to offer the car at a discounted rate. Dad had told him that he was not a rich man and that he had just begun to get work in films as a songwriter. He had requested the seller to reduce the price a bit. When the seller finally quoted a discounted price, Dad said he would buy the car for sure, but only the next day. He needed time to think about his decision. He confessed to the seller that he was unable to decide if it was okay to spend so much money on a car, a second-hand car at that, when his career had yet to take off.

The seller told him, 'Listen, brother, if you buy my car tomorrow, the price will be higher. I am not going to give you the discount tomorrow. I agreed to the special price because you are just starting out in your career. But the discounted price is valid only if you buy the car today! Also, if I get another and better offer today, I will not wait for you until tomorrow! So take it now or pay more tomorrow.'

Dad told the seller, 'You cannot force me to buy the car right away by offering me a discount that is valid only for today. And if that is your condition, then I am willing to buy the car at a higher price, but I will buy it only after this day and night have passed. It may not be a big decision for you to sell your car, but it's a huge decision for me to buy one. And so, I must think about it again, for which I need a night! Whatever be the cost of this delay.'

The very next day, 21 June 1966, Dad purchased the car, his first vehicle, at a higher price! He never regretted buying it on his own terms. My father believed that this Fiat car proved lucky for him, because he said he was flooded with work that year onwards, coinciding with the birth of my sister Kavita. We still have the car in our family—it was gifted to Kavita after he passed away in 2002.

After Dad had finished telling me the story about the Fiat, he said to me, 'Don't let the world ever rush you for their needs. If you have to be rushed, rush for your needs alone, or for the needs of your family . . . Believe in your values, believe in yourself.' The poem he wrote for his most beloved car:

Bakhshi hum yaaron ke yaar
Apni yaar hai Fiat car
Baaki sab kaarein bekaar.
Thi meri pehli chit-chor
Model 1964

Ab tak uss se mera pyaar.
Fiat mera latest romance
Sadkon par yeh karti dance
Tej hawaa jaisi raftaar.
Bakhshi hum yaaron ke yaar
Apni yaar hai Fiat car
Baaki sab kaarein bekaar.

* * *

One of Anand Bakshi's songs from *Ram Lakhan*, '*One two ka four, four two ka one, my name is Lakhan*', was interpreted by a columnist thus: *One two ka four* symbolizes the idea that to attain four-dimensional success in the world, one has to break the one-dimensional and two-dimensional rules. And *Four two ka one* refers to something you invest a lot in but which gives you far less returns than what you had expected.

The lyrics sound frivolous, but if you watch the film, you would understand that the columnist's interpretation of the lyrics is apt for the character played by Anil Kapoor. Another sign of the lyricist sticking to the director's brief of the story and character.

He once had to write a song about menstruation. About this song from *Aap Ki Kasam*, he said, 'Among the most challenging situations I was tasked with was when I was asked to write about an intimate and taboo subject in our culture. It was a "happy" situation between two lovers, and the girl had to convey to her husband why they couldn't get intimate today. Considering it was being sung on screen by superstars Rajesh Khanna and Mumtaz, I knew the song would get a wide audience and that a woman singer would sing it (Lataji). I had to publicly convey a subject that even family members are hush-hush about inside their homes, and movies are a family experience, even for me. I wrote, after much effort, "*Paas nahi aana, bhool nahi jana, tum ko saugandh hai ke aaj mohabbat bandh hai.*"'

Bakshi was a deeply philosophical lyricist. Take, for instance, one of his songs in *Aaya Sawan Jhoom Ke*, where he channels Mahatma

Gandhi's philosophy: *'Kissi ne kaha hai, mere doston, bura mat kaho, bura mat dekho, bura mat suno.'*

The poet Rumi said, 'The cure for pain, is in the pain.' Something similar is expressed in the song 'Aa Bataa Dein Ye Tujhe Kaise Jiya Jaata Hai' from *Dost*: *'Aa bataa dein, ke tujhe kaise jiya, jaata hai . . . Kaise nadaan hain woh, gham se anjaan hain jo, ranjh na hota agar, kya khushi ki thi kadar; dard khudh hai maseeha doston, dard se bhi dawaa ka doston, kaam liya jaata hai, maine bhi seekh liya, kaise jiya, jaata hai.'*

Bakshi was a great fan of Tagore. We had Tagore's photograph on the main wall of our living room for over four decades. Once, as usual, Dad was asked to sing one of his songs at a gathering of family and friends. He decided to sing an emotional song, from his film *Milan*, *'Aaj dil pe koi zor chalta nahin, muskurane lage the, magar ro pade.'* When he announced this, one of his close friends said, 'Bakshiji, don't sing a sad song. Sing us a happy song. It's a party.'

Dad replied, 'Rabindranath Tagore has said, "The happiest songs are the sad songs."' The gathering cheered at this, and he went on to regale us with one sad song after another, including his own favourites, 'Doli, Oh Doli' from *Rajput*, 'Duniya mein kitna gham hai' (*Amrit*) and 'Chingari Koi Bhadke' (*Amar Prem*). The latter was among his favourite songs.

Bakshi was well versed in scripture. The Bible says, 'Let that man first cast a stone who has not sinned.' In his song 'Yaar Humari Baat Suno' (*Roti*), Bakshi wrote, *'Iss paapan ko aaj saza denge hum milkar saare, lekin jo paapi na ho woh pehala patthar maare.'* Similarly, in a song from *Yudh* he quoted from the Bhagavad Gita, *'Danke pe chot padi hai, saamne maut khadi hai, Karan ne kaha Arjun se, na pyar jataa dushman se, yudh kar.'*

As he once said, 'It's not about making hit films or writing a hit script. Hits and flops are learnings. What really matters at the end of the run is the kind of person you become while going through the highs and lows of hits and flops. And the family and friends you earn and keep along the way. That's the best reward of life.'

10

2000–2002

'The Best News Is That I Am Alive'

Sometime in 2001, Dad suffered his first mild brain stroke and lost his speech partially. And it was because of my sister Suman that he could quickly regain his ability to speak. She would visit him daily and teach him to speak: they would slowly go over the English alphabet and then switch to numbers. Within a few weeks, he got his speech back. God bless her.

Dad's health issues, heart-related, began sometime in the '80s and resurfaced in the late '90s. In March 2002, when he was admitted to hospital for brain stroke, before slipping into a coma a few hours later, he said, 'Whatever happens in life, happens for our good. Have faith in God.' These were probably his last words to me.

When Dad needed a blood transfusion, we started looking for donors. His was a rare blood type: B negative. We put up posters, sent out SMSes and emails, to friends, acquaintances, relations. The very first person to volunteer was the ward boy who had been looking after Dad. He loved to sing and would entertain Dad by singing his songs. Another stranger who showed up for donating blood said that he felt honoured giving his blood to his childhood idol. Such touching moments made us realize that this was what he had earned in life— true affection that money cannot buy.

On 30 March 2002, Dad passed away.

* * *

Just as Our Soul Is Immortal, So Should Be Our Work

After Dad's passing, I began to sleep in his room, so that Mom wouldn't feel too lonely. Subsequently, after we found our footing and the household began to 'normalize', my brother and I had to take possession of his personal belongings. When I opened his cupboard, the first thing that hit me like a sudden storm was the scent associated with him and the memories triggered by it. His clothes still carried the leftover fragrance of his perfumes. His soap in the bathroom, Lifebuoy, was still exactly the way he had left it. I did not have the courage to get rid of even his soap.

Gradually, we began to give away some of his belongings to the needy and donated some to worthy institutions. When I opened his wallet, I found a few photographs of his Bansi Wale, Sai Baba, Vaishno Devi Mata, Ganeshji, Saraswati Mata and some others. Among the other fascinating items was a Rs 100 note gifted to him by film-maker and dear friend Subhash Ghai; a Rs 100 note gifted to him by my brother Rajesh from his first earnings; and a quote from the Bhagavat Gita:

> Rare indeed is the human birth. The human body is like a boat, the first and the foremost use of which is to carry us across oceans of life and death, to the shores of immortality. The Guru is the boatman, and God is the favourable wind. If with such means as these, man does not strive to cross the ocean of life and death, he is indeed spiritually dead.

To this, he had added the line, 'Just as our soul is immortal, so should be our work.'

* * *

There Will Always Be a Bill

Dad would throw this advice at us children now and then: 'If you think you have got something for nothing, you have not received the bill yet.' When asthma began to overwhelm him in 2001, he needed to breathe using the oxygen provided via an external cylinder. He would say, 'This asthma is the bill I am receiving for not adhering to the advice given to me time and again by my family, doctors and friends, smoking is injurious to health. If only I had known then how much I would suffer, I would never have let even anyone else smoke.'

Besides the asthma, he suffered from loneliness in the last two years of his life. Despite having the whole family next to him, Dad felt I didn't spend enough time with him. He was right, and I am sorry for that. I now give my siblings more quality time.

Back in 2002, in a published feature on Anand Bakshi, some journalist wrote that it seemed to him Bakshi was alone or lonely, and that his family did not share in his success. Though the writer has a right to his opinions, I think it is important to clear the air. Bakshi must have felt alone in his success. But that's the human condition—each one of us essentially feels lonely at times, whether we are at the top, in the middle or at the bottom. Yet in the last two years of his life, Dad was with his family, his two doctor friends and his film-maker friends, like Subhash Ghai and Sunil Dutt. All stood by him throughout.

'Sunil Dutt arranged doctors for a second opinion during my prolonged sickness. Subhash Ghai became my pillar and backbone at the worst hour of my life, when my own walls had begun to crumble. He arranged Ayurvedic doctors at his own cost to cure me, as he thought allopathy medicines are only ruining my health further. My friend and director Mohan Kumar, advocate Shyam Keswani and my Ustaad Chhitar Mal's son too would visit me at home to cheer me up.'

Success and failure, both are very often solo journeys. Except that in success, we have the support of people, whereas in suffering and pain, few stand by us. But the ones who matter most, eventually, in our life's journey are not only those who cut birthday cakes and popped champagne bottles with us, but also those who spent the nights next to us in hospital wards or in freezing corridors outside ICUs, taking turns to visit, running from pillar to post to find blood donors, ordering rare medicines from abroad—which we all, his family and close friends, did for Dad.

Dad adored his family, and we adored him, in spite of our differences, shortcomings and flaws. Each one of us (his wife, four children and two sons-in-law) was dependable, and remains so to date, and he would have been the happiest for that. In the last year of his life, Dad had told my brother and me, 'I have never sent you all on a world tour. When I will be back home from the hospital this time and am well again, I want to send you all on a world tour because each one of you has taken so much care of me over the last one year and more.' We had never asked for such a trip, but he really wanted to send us, and the thought alone was a big reward for us children.

* * *

'My Life, My Work, My Terms'

Anand Bakshi's fans, friends and relatives say that he passed away too soon. However, he departed exactly when he wanted, according to his wish. It was important for Dad to live life on his own terms and to keep working until his last: 'I want to die with my boots on.'

He wished to be busy writing songs till his dying day. He wrote nine songs in the two months before he died, for directors Anil Sharma and Subhash Ghai. The ex-fauji had always wished a death of honour and not an existence that dwindled, through retirement or disease, to nothing.

'I want to leave the industry before the industry leaves me.'

Geetkaar Anand Bakshi wrote his last song, for producer Subhash Ghai and composer Anu Malik, in February 2002. It was '*Bulleh Shah tere ishq nachaya, wah ji wah tere ishq nachaya*'. He wrote the song in a fever, confined to his bed, covered in three warm blankets; he would shiver from the fever and weakness, and was breathless due to the asthma. That same week, he was admitted in hospital and never returned home.

Yash Chopra's *Mohabbatein* and Subhash Ghai's *Yaadein* released in 2000 and 2001 respectively. Both films had great songs, composed by top music directors, and featured big stars in lead roles. In 2002 and 2003, a total of eight films were released for which Bakshi had written songs.

Dad never wanted to live as a dependant. Except for Mom, he did not depend on anyone else. One month before he died, he could not walk, eat or sleep without help and support. A week before his death, he went into a semi-coma. A day before, he went into a deep coma, and the doctors said he might have suffered brain damage.

I remember a doctor friend's words to me on the morning Dad was declared brain dead: 'Your father is no longer a poet. Meaning, even if he comes out of the coma, he'll never know who he was.' This happened at around 10 a.m. Dad died that same evening, at around 8.30 p.m.

He lived as a dependant for less than a month, which I think was a blessing for a man who had always wanted to remain independent. In his last year, I prayed daily for his good health and long life. His last day—when my doctor friend told me that Dad was most probably brain dead and that it was perhaps the ventilator that was keeping him 'alive'—was the only time I prayed for his death, and his Bansi Wale heard my prayer, I suppose.

I believe Dad was a lucky, blessed man. He never had to ask for work post the late '60s, thanks to his Bansi Wale. He worked hard, played hard, ate to his heart's content and rarely cut down on his favourite foods because of his medical condition. He lived on his own terms, and he left on his terms.

He managed to achieve so much more than what he aspired for— as outlined in his 'Aim in Life' note—because of his Bansi Wale and his guiding belief, that our deeds are as important as destiny, which he mentions in his personal diary: 'There is something inside me superior to my circumstances, stronger than every situation of life.'

* * *

Dad's Diary

Now, I am going to share some pertinent and significant notes Dad made in his personal diary, for which I took the permission of my siblings. I am not going to comment on every note that I am sharing here chronologically. I decided not to share some of the notes because everyone deserves their privacy, especially ones who are no longer around to explain or defend their words and deeds.

1982

20 August: 'That's why God has saved me today, to love you all too. Anyway, this is the best card I've ever received. Also, thanks to Dr Gandhi, Dr Sharad Panday, Dr S.G. Gokhale and Dr Sharad Apte.' (The note was written by Dad on a get-well-soon card we children gifted to him after he had just recovered from his first heart attack.)

1997

1 May: 'My children and Kamla don't like me eating paan and smoking. I must stop for their sake, for my children's sake, as I love them.' (Thereafter, Dad made many promises to himself and us that he will quit paan and cigarette, but he failed to deliver on them.)

2000

4 January: 'Time is running out for me, and I have yet to fulfil so many duties as a writer and father.'

15 May: 'Today again I am feeling weak and sick. I smoked three cigarettes also. Do you want to go to hospital again? No, I will not go to hospital. Rather die.'

29 May: 'I stopped smoking but back to chewing tobacco. Bakhshi, you will suffer.'

29 September: 'Dr Sharad Apte and S.G. Gokhale and family have always been helpful to me and my family, god bless him. Thank you, Dr Apte and Dr Gokhale.'

31 December: 'Next year, I will write down my Achievements. I will narrate my life story to Sunil Dutt and Subhash Ghai. I had narrated my story to Yash Chopra many years ago; he was impressed by the naval mutiny incident at Karachi and Bombay, and said that one day he would make a film on the subject.'

31 December: 'God please help me and let me help myself. 2001 has to be a healthy year for me. No more bad habits. Time has changed so much during the last thirty-five years.'

2001

1 January: 'I swear by Mitra (Maaji) last time to change my destiny. Whatever happens in 2001, I'll live and I will celebrate. I won't be a sick man. God help me. I won't be a sick man. First step, stop smoking as a habit from today.'

17 February: 'Kamla, I am losing a war after having almost won it. No, I will not surrender. I will give myself a last chance from tomorrow. I will win.'

(Date unspecified): 'To save myself and kill myself at the same time. How is this possible? Either I can save myself or kill myself. I think this is a compulsion of all my fears, phobias and feelings. But can this change? No. Yes, if I command myself and leave all this nonsense, I can conquer the feelings and suffering. But am I . . . No, I am a lucky man.'

30 March: 'One cigarette today.'

31 March: 'Last three cigarettes.'

4 April: 'Last cigarette for Subhash Ghai.'

1 May: 'I am smoking. I am creating worries, tension for myself. I am going against the law of nature. I am committing suicide if I continue, I could become invalid for life. I would die if I continue. But I want to save myself, and live. It is very strange. I want to save myself, and I am killing myself at the same time. God, please help me live. I don't want to sacrifice my work, name, fame, my wife, family, for these bad habits. Bakhshi, do not lose a game you have always won. Do it for my Kamla and children.'

> 'Mujhko chuna halaat ne, ya maine chuna halaat ko? Bhagwan Bansi
> Wale meri madat karega; himmat-e-marda, maddat-e-Khuda.'

15 May: 'I am again feeling weak and sick. I don't want to go to hospital again. I would rather die . . . But I want to live, write more songs, my family.'

18 May: 'In the last almost forty years, today is the first day of no paan, no cigarette. Because last night I had a *real* asthma attack.'

29 May: 'I stopped smoking, but again started chewing paan. Bakhshi, you will suffer!'

3 June: 'Again I have started to eat tobacco in the same way perhaps. I am waiting for another stroke? Within this week this has to change.'

11 June: 'But as she and children left for Jaipur, I missed them all very much—I cried a little also. I don't know when they come next year if I would be here or not. Dady.' (He would spell 'Daddy' as 'Dady'. This was written when my sister Kavita [Rani] and her children returned to their home in Jaipur after their annual summer vacation. He wasn't around when they returned the next year.)

15 July: 'My anxieties, worries, paan, overeating habits are not stopping. I should make myself stop these bad habits.'

20 July: 'Today my BP is high. I had some discussions with Gogi and Daboo. I am tense. Tomorrow is my birthday party. People are coming home. Everything is arranged, more than enough. Why am I tense? It's going to be a perfect party. I am not alone. Whole family is here, helpers are there, and our friends are coming. Pappi, Vinay, the kids are coming. What is this fear? This has become a habit for me, to create worries. Am I giving a party and spending so much money to be tense and worried? No, I am going to enjoy my birthday . . . They are running a special picture on me on my birthday. People are there. Whisky is there. Food is there. What else do I want?'

On his birthday, after welcoming our guests at around 9–10 p.m., I withdrew to my own room to complete some film-making work. The past year had been a bad one for Daddy—his asthma was getting worse, and he had been in and out of hospital at least two times that year. We were all stressed. I was stressed because I was just three years into the film-making profession, working as an assistant to Subhash Ghai, on his films *Taal* and *Yaadein*, and I had just been through a failed business and a divorce. My finances, self-worth, confidence and self-esteem, had taken a massive hit. Dad, Mom, my brother Gogi, sisters Rani and Pappi, and close friends Rohit, Ambika, and a few others stood by me. Daddy entered my room around 11.30 p.m. and asked me to join the 'party', the celebrations. He said he wanted us to hear a poem he had written for this occasion. I told him I was occupied with work and would join them soon. But he had noticed that I was not as busy with work as I was stressed and depressed due to my own life situation. He told me, 'Beta, this is going to be my last birthday. I will not be around next year. *Agle saal iss time par panchi pinjare se udd gaya hoga* (The bird [soul] will have escaped the cage [body] by this time next year).' He departed next year, on 30 March 2002.

This was the poem he recited to us on the night of 20 July 2001, the eve of his seventy-second birthday:

Ikhattar Saal Guzare
Bade behaal guzare.
Sune kothe pe mujre
Likhe geeton ke mukhde.
Hue iss dil ke tukde
Suno Bakhshi ke dukhde:
Kahin lakhon mein ek hoon
Main bas ek nagrik hoon.
Yahi hai naam mera
Hai charcha aam mera.
Hukumat ka main pyara
Magar gurbatt ka mara.
Yunhi din saal guzare
Bade behaal guzare.
Kabhi machiss nahi thi

Kabhi cigarette nahi thi.
Kabhi dono the lekin
Mujhe fursat nahin thi.
Kabhi fursat milli toh
Ijaazat hi nahi thi.
Ijaazat mil gayee toh
Yeh daulat hi nahi thi.
Yeh daulat mil gayee toh
Woh himmat hi nahi thi.
Kabhi himmat bhi ki toh
Woh chaahat hi nahi thi.
Kabhi chaahat nahi thi
Kabhi kismat nahi thi.
Kabhi kuch tha adhura
Mukkamall kuch nahi tha.
Rahaa sab kuch barabar
Zyaada kum nahi tha.
Judaai toh nahi thi
Magar sangam bhi nahi tha.
Tabiyat ke mutabik
Kabhi mausam nahi tha.
Kabhi botal nahi thi
Kabhi yeh gham nahi tha.
Mujhe aaj kuch na kehana
Mera dil thikhane hai na.

That night, Dad also he recited his poems 'Rawalpindi' and 'Main Koi Barf Nahi Hoon', and sang the song '*Asa hun, turr jaan aaye ke din raine gaye thode . . . likhne wale ne likh daale*' from the film *Arpan*. It was perhaps his way of informing us that he would leave us soon.

28 July: 'My friend Subhash Ghai has become a big man. I am happy for him. He is a good friend, good producer, respects me.' (He wrote

this hearing the good news that Ghai's Mukta Arts was now a public limited company.)

12 August: 'I must control my diet and emotions. Why suffer when I can enjoy life? I must accept that I cannot smoke or eat like in my younger days.'

Our family doctor, Dr S.G. Gokhale, once shared with me this amusing anecdote about Dad:

Bakshiji called me saying that he could not raise his right hand. I rushed to your house and found that he was almost going into paralysis. I examined him, and we decided to go to the hospital immediately. But he said he was feeling a little better and asked me to wait a minute. He told your mother to make him one paan. I scolded him, 'Bakshiji, you should not eat *tambaaku ka* paan now, it will worsen your condition.' But he went ahead and even smoked a cigarette! I was panting with anger, not knowing what was going to happen to this stubborn man. The responsibility was mine as I was also his family doctor and friend. Then Bakshiji had the paan and said to me, 'Doctor Sa'ab, paan emergency *mein kaam aata hai* (a paan comes in handy during an emergency).'

We left for the hospital. As we entered the hospital lobby, he collapsed! Luckily, the ICU was right there, so he was revived soon. Happily, he returned home after a few weeks. What your mother told me later was, 'Bakshi Sa'ab *roz subah ek paan banwate hein aur usse apne paas rakhte hein aur din bhar usse khaate nahin, aur shaam ko usse phek dete hain. Roz aisa karte hain* (He orders a paan every morning, keeps it with himself all day and throws it away in the evening).' Your mother was annoyed and, wondered why he asks her to make a paan every day when he does not eat it. I asked Bakshiji why he does that. He replied, 'Doctor Sa'ab, I told you, emergency mein paan kaam aata hai. That day I would have died at home, but because I had a paan, I reached the hospital walking on my own, and in a few weeks I came home alive. So, although I do not eat paan, I make one every day for such an emergency. *Paan hai toh jaan hai!*'

During his long hospitalization, sometime in April 2001, and later in September 2001, he would sing songs at the request of the ward sisters, nurses, doctors and even sweepers. He was a born entertainer.

Sometime in 2001, Anand Bakshi confided in his well-wisher and *mureed*, the lyricist Sameer Anjaan, 'I know I am going to die soon. I don't fear or regret dying. I do regret that I still have so many songs within that I wish I could write or give to my family or to a good lyricist like you for keeps. However, I regret that since they came with me, so they will have to leave with me.'

'*Mera sab kuch mere geet re, geet bina kaun mera meet re*'

—*Zindagi*

Back in 1984, when he was asked which song he considered his best work, Anand Bakshi said, 'I have not achieved much as yet. I am yet to write my best songs. I hope to be able to do that soon. Hope never dies. Hope dies only with death.'

24 September: Dad's last note/letter to me: 'Dear Daboo, love you. God bless you. How are you? Look after Mother, Brother Gogi.'

30 November: This was written after he returned home from the hospital: 'The best news is that I am alive. And they say this feeling is the happiest of all. God somehow gave you back the empty paper of life; now start writing. Tagore had said, "I never sang the song I came to sing. I have been busy stringing and unstringing my instrument." Stop this wastage of time. Sing. Sing. Sing. We all are actors; we perform on stage and go. All came, all went. Kings, fakirs, poets, the rich and the powerful. Why do you always want to live on this stage

of life? How boring this must be. When this body becomes useless, a source of tension for you and the others. Relax now. Truth is God. Enjoy for some time. Because the new body, new responsibilities, are being set up. Be ready for everything—New Nando. Anand Prakash Bakhshi.'

'Jagat musafirkhana, laga hai aana jana'

—Balika Badhu

2002

3 January: 'Oh My God. I don't know how what when all happened. I don't know how to address God. What name to give him Bhagwaan, Ram, Allah, Christ, Guru Nanak I will say Shri Krishna. I had a long and bad attack of asthma. Dabu gave me the nebulizer. I slept peacefully. I woke up at 11 p.m. Had sweet dish custard and no medicines and slept. Woke up. I called Gogi, Kamla and shared the news. A feeling I had at that time: God said to me, your troubles are over. You have suffered enough. From today, you are free of these illnesses and symptoms, except for the problems of daily living. Oh God Krishanji, Bansi Wale, I have said thanks always and not only for my *dukh* or *sukh*. I think I am improving daily.'

8 January: 'I went for a walk in the garden outside my house and fell down and injured myself. Since September 2001, I have had a very bad time, but God saved me. I am alive. I have to win this battle of health and become the same man once again, Anand Prakash. Bless me, God. The happiest and best feeling is that I am alive.'

31 January: '6.15 a.m. I dreamt I am sick, sleeping, but God is watching me, smiling, a satisfied look on His face. I asked God what is happening to me. God said, "Well, this is what I dreamt for you. I am sorry. If you want to be happy, accept my wishes, and be thankful to

life, death, let all the miracles happen happily." I agreed and said, "God, thinking your way. I am happy. Fully awake on my bed. Bombay, at Coste Belle. Your Son. Anand Bakhshi.'"

11 February: '1.30 a.m. I dreamt I woke up to find two people carrying my body, and everything had changed. My name had changed, some smoke, my whole body had changed. All my pain had gone. I cannot show my body to anyone as it is not there any longer.'

There are no diary entries after this date.

* * *

'*Aap ke anurodh pe, main yeh geet sunata hoon*'

When Dad was in a state of coma, twice within the span of a year—he would never return from the second one—we played to him his own songs on his personal mono cassette player, through a pair of headphones, in the hope that his lyrics, which have inspired so many, will inspire him, the author, the creator of the same. We would play the songs that he loved to sing—songs like 'Chingari Koi Bhadke' and 'Gaadi Bula Rahi Hai' among many others. We were hopeful that he was aware of surroundings and that his own inspiring words will awaken him, motivate him to return to our world. It was a chance, a hope, a prayer, that we siblings and our mother counted on. We failed to revive him, but we believe that he knew what we were doing for him, and that he felt loved during his last moments.

From his diary, an earlier, undated entry:

'Happenings mean life. Life brought me into this world of happenings. Death will take me back where nothing happens. Just nothing. It is only after death that nothing happens. After death, a person goes into nothingness. No feelings, no sound. I too will remain in that atmosphere of nothingness for a while. Then again, something will happen, and I will get a new life, new name, new game, new people around me, new childhood, new body, each and everything new. What is there to worry about? Nothing. Life and death are my permanent companions, as rebirth is a fact. This coming and going will go on forever. Life and death, both are very beautiful. Life is work, nothing else. Death is rest, nothing else. Without death, life has no beginning, no ending, no meaning.

'Why run away from death? Death is nowhere, yet everywhere, with you, within you. Accept that I cannot live forever. When we fear death, we doubt God. Do I doubt God? No. I believe in God. I am myself a little proof of God. He is the seven seas. I am a drop of water. I am from Him, for Him.'

Tributes

'Deewane tere naam ke, khade hain dil tham ke'

Pyarelal Sharma (of Laxmikant–Pyarelal)

We first met Bakshiji properly, in Kalyanji–Anandji's music room at Peddar Road, we were Kalyanji–Anandji's music assistants. Bakshiji was the most punctual among us. Punctuality and discipline were his prime qualities. He was not a slave of his moods and desires, nor of the ambience. He delivered as and when required, wherever he was, whether in their sitting room or at the recording studio, no excuses ever. Never.

Bakshiji would work out the basic mukhda or antara of the song immediately on hearing the story, and the next day he would deliver us the complete song with more than the needed number of verses. Then it would be the director's, and sometimes even the composers', headache what to keep and what to literally sacrifice, because we could not use more than three verses. I still believe that Bakshiji came here to become a singer and music composer, and writing was just his hobby. But look at the legacy he leaves behind as a writer! He very rightly said, *'Zindagi ke safar mein guzar jaate hain jo mukam, woh phir nahi aate.'* I miss him.

Dharmendra (Singh Deol)

I called him 'King'. We worked in nearly 70–71 films. Laxmikant–
Pyarelal, Rafi and he gifted us a wonderful song in *Pratiggya* (1975),
'Main Jat Yamla Pagla Deewana'. *Aaj bhi bajta hai yeh gaana.* Writing
was effortless for him. Back in the 1970s, in front of S.D. Burman and
me, he wrote this verse in less than five minutes, '*Yeh dil deewana hai,
dil toh deewana hai, deewana dil hai yeh, dil deewana.*' The brief from
Ramesh Saigal, the director of *Ishq Par Zor Nahin*, was to write a song
with the word 'dil' appearing four or five times. Bakshi Sa'ab was not
just a lyricist. He was a poet. I miss him dearly.*

Yash Chopra

I would meet Bakshiji often at film functions and film parties. By
then, he was already a very successful lyrics writer. He also loved to
sing and sang well. One day I was reintroduced to him by my lyrics
writer Sahir. Sahir was not only my lyrics writer but also my dear
friend, and he told me, 'Use Anand Bakshi for lyrics someday in
your film. He also writes well.' I was surprised, that my own lyrics
writer Sahir Sa'ab was recommending another lyrics writer. I was very
happy with Sahir Sa'ab writing lyrics in my films, and I had not asked
him to recommend to me another lyrics writer. Yet he did! And he
recommended Anand Bakshi.

The best thing about Bakshiji—even though we both were
established professionals by the time we met sometime in the 1980s,
with Sahir Sa'ab, and even before that, on and off, at parties—was that
he never ever asked me for an opportunity to write songs in my films.
I think Bakshiji knew that Sahir Sa'ab was my favourite lyrics writer

---

* Immediately after I had met Dharmendraji, on my way out of his house, I met
his brother, Ajit Singh Deol, the producer of *Pratiggya*. He told me, 'Bakshi Sa'ab
was not a geeetkar. *Woh humare pir the.* Some of his songs are the words of a pir, a
spiritual guide.'

and my dear friend too, and Bakshiji honoured and respected that relationship we shared. I can say Bakshiji was among the good human beings I have met, and the number one lyrics writer. Of course, there were many good poets and lyrics writers, but there will be only one lyrics writer-cum-poet like Anand Bakshi.

One day, a big producer wanted me to direct a film for him—the music was by R.D. Burman and the producer was Gulshan Rai. He—or was it Pancham?—suggested to me, that we should sign Anand Bakshi Sa'ab for the lyrics in my film. Consequently, I met Bakshiji and he gladly agreed to work in my film as lyrics writer without asking me any questions about why Sahir was not writing for the film.

However, when I returned home, I felt guilty and very bad. I thought Sahir Sa'ab was also a very good songwriter who had been my very good friend for many years. Therefore, I thought I should continue to work with Sahir Sa'ab, even though Sahir Sa'ab himself had once told me to work with Bakshiji also. I decided to go back to Bakshi Sa'ab and tell him I was sorry that I wouldn't be able to work with him. Embarrassed, I approached Bakshiji hesitantly and apologized profusely for going back on my word to him. I honestly told Bakshiji that I wanted to remain loyal to my very dear friend and very talented writer Sahir Sa'ab, so I could not use his (Bakshiji's) talent in my film, even though it was I who had approached him.

Bakshiji was extremely graceful and happy that I wanted to continue working with Sahir Sa'ab, even though he and I had a deal from the day before. I think the reason was that Sahir Sa'ab had given Bakshiji good advice on songwriting and had also introduced him to some good producers and directors when Bakshiji was desperately looking for a foothold in the profession in the '50s and '60s. Bakshiji never forgot Sahir Sa'ab's help, I think.

Surprisingly, Bakshiji told me that even if we were not to work together in this film or any other, we should remain friends. Bakshi Sa'ab never spoke ill of any other rival writers, or of people he did not work with, or of those who did not want to work with him. He was always quiet, did his job quietly, and then he would leave once his work was done. Even when we became friends over the many films we did together, he never indulged in any unnecessary chatter or gossip. He would never hang around; he would leave immediately after the song was done.

It was only when God took Sahir Sa'ab away from us that I approached Bakshiji for my film. *Chandni* was my first film with him. And what songs, what lyrics he gifted my film and our films thereafter! Unforgettable contribution! I was very worried *Chandni* would not do well. He saw the preview of the film and told me I had made a superhit. His sense of story was excellent.

Bakshiji would write songs within minutes for me. Sometimes he wrote songs in his car, travelling from his house in Bandra to my house in Juhu, in a span of fifteen minutes. Sometimes he wrote verses for me in less than four minutes while I would be on hold on the telephone. When we would get stuck during a recording of a song and I felt a verse or word needed to be changed, I would call him, and he would never say no, never tell me that he'd call tomorrow. There and then, he wrote and changed the words or lines for me! Such a professional! Such was Bakshiji's talent, speed, depth, dedication and enthusiasm. He never questioned or fussed with me about why I wanted anything changed even after I had approved it earlier. He always delivered on every occasion that arose, any time, any day.

Once, when he was admitted in Nanavati Hospital for getting a pacemaker, I went to meet him there. He told me he had thought of some new verses for a song in *Chandni* which he had already delivered to me. I had never asked him to improve on what he had already written. So, he was thinking of his directors and producers even while he was being treated for his heart ailment in a hospital! Where are such people, such dedication, such talent, such sincerity, such enthusiasm, today?

Even today, Bakshi Sa'ab remains unforgettable for me, and for my son Aditya.

Lata Mangeshkar*

Bakshiji was the only one who would compliment me by saying in
Punjabi 'Wah ji wah!' whenever we met at the studio after recording
our songs. Some of his songs that I have sung come to my memory
right away: 'Jaane kyun log, mohabbat karte hain', 'Baaghon mein bahar
hai, kaliyon pe nikhaar hai, tumko mujhse pyar hai', 'Tu mere saamne,
main tere saamne, tujhko dekhoon ke pyar karoon', 'Tere mere honton pe,
meethe meethe geet mitwa', 'Pyar teri, pehli nazar ko salaam'.

He never interfered with anyone during recordings. He was a
very quiet man and one of the few lyricists who made it a point to
attend all his recordings and, when necessary, confidently suggest
changes in expressions to even experienced singers who he thought
had not comprehended his words completely or were pronouncing
them incorrectly. When I was recording 'Tere mere honton pe, meethe
meethe geet mithwa' for Chandni, he came up to me and asked me to
pronounce the word 'meethe' hard, with a strong 'thh' instead of a soft
one. His suggestion made a world of difference to the song! While he
was recording his first song as a singer, I was pleasantly surprised to
learn that he sang like a professional, because sometimes new singers
feel nervous singing with me for the first time. He sang well and I
think he had made the dhun too.

When I won the Padma Vibhushan in 2001, he presented me
with a poem that he had written as a tribute to me. He was not well, I
think, yet he came to see me at the event and gave the poem to me after
the event was over, when I walked down the stage. I was very touched
by his affection and gesture.

Yeh gulshan mein baad-e-saba gaa rahi hai
Ke parbat pe kaali ghata gaa rahi hai

---

* Lataji has sung the maximum number of songs written by Dad. I have not done
a complete count, but till October 1990, she had sung 679 songs, for 309 films,
written by him.

Yeh jharno ne paida kiya hai tarannum
Ke nadiya koi geet sa gaa rahi hai

Yeh Mahiwaal ko yaad karti hai Sohni
Ke Meera bhajan Shyam ka gaa rahi hai

Mujhe jaane kya kya gumaan ho rahey hain
Nahi aur koi, Lata gaa rahi hai

Yunn hi kaash gaati rahein yeh hamesha
Dua aaj khud yeh dua gaa rahi hai

Subhash Ghai

During a song sitting for *Meri Jung*, I suggested an expression to Bakshiji, '*Zindagi har kadam ek jung hai*,' and within a second he responded, '*Jeet jayenge hum, agar tu sangh hai, zindagi har kadam ik nayi jung hai*.' I knew we had our song's mukhda.

One evening, on 3 August 1984, I was with him, and we were working on the songs of *Karma*. He narrated the lyrics to me, '*Dil diya hai jaan bhi denge, aye watan tere liye; har karam apna karenge, aye watan tere liye*.' The moment Bakshiji finished reading out the heart-rending lyrics, I got emotional and handed him a Rs 100 note as a token of appreciation. I wrote a few lines in appreciation and handed it to him: 'On the pen of Anand Bakshi. With Compliments, the pen of Subhash Ghai.'*

Bakshiji had a habit of preserving things he was emotionally attached to, but I didn't know that he had actually kept that note till the end of his life. I was overwhelmed. These days, many things are

---

* Twenty-nine years after this affectionate exchange and eleven years after Dad's death, I discovered this note neatly tucked into his last wallet. He had never parted with this note of appreciation.

about money and nothing is more important than your film crossing the Rs 100 crore mark and more. But this incident reminds me of a time when even Rs 100 was most valuable and sentiments were treasured. By keeping the currency note with him till his death, Anand Bakshi has given me a compliment I will cherish for the rest of my life.

Bakshiji and I did fourteen films together: *Gautam Govinda, Karz, Krodhi, Vidhaata, Hero, Meri Jung, Karma, Ram Lakhan, Saudagar, Khal Nayak, Shikhar, Pardes, Taal, Yaadein.* Few people realize that it's the lyricist who writes around forty-five minutes of a 150-minute film. It is lyrics that give our films repeat value, and nostalgia. Fans recollect film names from songs, actors are elevated by the songs they sing, singers are recognized from the lyrics they sing. So, lyricists must be paid their due, monetarily and in terms of credit.

He survived in this industry, which is full of paradoxical and ironical situations, without controversy. His best quality was his discipline—he never delayed a song. Another thing: sometimes, some singers would ask me if I loved the way they sang the song, but the person who wrote these songs, Anand Bakshi, never asked me this question. He was perhaps secure in the knowledge that he had done justice to his work.

Anand Bakshi's songs remain among the best documents of Indian cinema. His songs will be dissected and studied, evaluated by students of screenplay, lyrics and music, in future music universities. His demise is the cruelest tragedy of my life. Bakshiji's expertise went a long way in rendering my projects successful. He should be awarded a Bharat Ratna.

Bakshiji would listen to the film's story so keenly that he would internalize the entire story. He knew the story better than even the director himself. In every film, I would have a theme song that had the basic story. Once Bakshiji had written a song this comprehensive, I would use that as a guide to shoot the movie thereafter. I did that in *Vidhata*, after he wrote the outstanding taqdeer versus tadbeer song, 'Haathon ki chand lakeeron ka . . .' It's my favourite song, and the one from our first film together, *Gautam Govinda*, 'Ik ritu aaye, ik ritu jaaye.' Yet another best thing about him, *unke gaane bikte the lekin woh bikaau nahi the.* Anand Bakshi's songs were for sale, not he; Bakshiji never compromised his values for work. An honest and precious man.

I would realize the real depth of his words only at the time of shooting, and usually when I was explaining the words to the artists. He wrote his last song—'*Bulleh Shah tere Ishq Nachaya, wah ji wah tere ishq nachaya*'—for my film. When he wrote it, he was in bed, with 101 fever, covered with three warm blankets, shivering, breathless due to the asthma, and with a low hemoglobin count of seven. That same week he was admitted in hospital, and he . . . never returned home. The loss of Bakshiji, the greatest lyrical legend, left us with only one sound. Silence.*

Shakti Samanta

Bakshiji had a talent of writing lyrics and composing the accompanying tunes while penning the words. He would sing his songs sometimes even better than the way they were rendered by singers. He would regale us with his poker-faced sense of humour and his songs at parties.†

J. Om Prakash

I liked to discuss my stories and screenplays in detail with Bakshiji during our song sittings, because he had a good sense of human

---

* Mr Ghai's tribute for Anand Bakshi ('disciplined, proactive') reminds me of a quality of Dad's that perhaps inspired me too in my formative years. He would never sit idle. If a song had to be delivered after a month, he wrote it anyway. And if he was idle, he would clean the house furniture and once that was done, he would reply to every single fan mail. He valued his fans and listeners as much as the producers who hired him to write.

† Anand Bakshi's first brand-new imported car, a Chevrolet Bel Air, was gifted to him by Shakti Samanta after the box-office success of *Aradhana*, but Bakshi insisted that he pay for it and would not accept it as a gift. Shakti Da graciously obliged.

emotions and would always give me very good suggestions. He would hear the story very keenly. He was genuinely interested in stories and situations that challenged him and provoked him deeply to write better lyrics. After he heard the story of *Aap Ki Kasam*, he remembered that one of his good friends had left his wife because he suspected she was having an extramarital affair. After a few years, the man realized he had been mistaken and went to apologize to her and wanted to remarry her. But she had moved on with another person and had remarried. The man committed suicide. And soon, Bakshiji came up with the lyrics, '*Zindagi ke safar mein guzar jaate hain jo mukaam, woh phir nahi aate.*' That song was so well written for the story, screenplay and characters that it did the job of two scenes I had already shot, so I got rid of these scenes during the edit. This song has helped me in my personal life too.

When I gave him the situation in *Aaye Din Bahaar Ke*, I told him to write what people really feel when they are betrayed or abandoned but don't express it. Deep down, we curse anyone who harms us. He wrote the most outstanding and as yet unmatched curse song, '*Mere dushman, tu meri, dosti ko tarse,*' in just about two hours.

Tony Juneja

Bakshi Sa'ab would usually come in his 1964 Fiat at six o'clock sharp in the evening to Raju's [music composer Rajesh Roshan] house, with a tobacco filled paan and a 555 cigarette packet, and we all would sit to think about the song. He had two other latest imported cars yet preferred to travel in his first car, the Fiat, even to film premieres. One evening, as usual, he was smoking his 555, and began humming a song, the lyrics with a tune—'*Pardesiya, ye sach hai piya, sab kehete hain toone, mera dil le liya.*' We were all surprised, but it sounded great to all of us. Raju and his musicians got all charged up and played along with Bakshi Sa'ab. The remaining three verses he wrote in front of all of us, in fifteen minutes, while chewing his paan and smoking his 555, taking very deep puffs.

It was he who was responsible for Amitabh Bachchan singing in films. When he wrote 'Mere Paas Aao, Mere Doston', he suggested, 'Why not make Amitabh sing this song in the film? The actor singing in his own voice will make the song sound more intimate, especially since he is singing with children.' It was to be Amitabh's first playback song in films.

Bakshiji was writing for everybody, so many producers, never believed in 'camps' or favoured any film clan, and yet he never let us down when we needed songs within a few days or hours; such was his professionalism and speed! One must learn from him that everybody's money is important and has value. So you should not and cannot let anybody down ever. Service before self and with a smile. You must adjust with everyone and deliver to everyone. He would tell me, 'My songs' rhythm will always sound like a heartbeat. I have written some songs tuned to the metre of my heartbeat. My songs will beat just as our heart beats. There was and will be no one like him.

Rajkumar Barjatya

When Bakshiji wrote the verse *'Jhil mil sitaaron ka aangan hoga, rim jhim barasta saawan hoga'* for *Jeevan Mrityu*, I politely objected, reasoning that one could not see stars if it was raining, as the sky would be covered with rain clouds. Bakshiji replied, 'Do not go by the words literally. Do not go so deep into what I have written. Think of what is being said like a poet, because the situation of this song is romance. Further, on close observation you will realize I have played with two letters, "N" and "M". There is the letter "M" in "jhilmil" and "N" in "aangan hoga". There is an "M" in "rim jhim", and an "N" in "saawan hoga". It is the play of the sounds of "N" and "M" that I want you to hear, which will make this song a pleasure to hear and sing, and thus will make the song popular.' I can say he was right. The song was a super-duper hit.

Bakshiji would write at least six verses for every song he wrote for our films, even though we wanted just three. When he met me the first time in 1967 for *Taqdeer*, he introduced himself simply as an ex-fauji who liked to write songs, as though he was a newcomer. He never mentioned that he was THE songwriter of the superhit *Jab Jab Phool Khile* and of other hits like *Mehndi Lagi Mere Haath, Himalay Ki God Mein, Aaye Din Bahaar Ke, Phool Bane Angaare, Mr. X In Bombay, Aasra, Devar, Chhota Bhai, Farz*. So humble!

The simple words he used in his songs was a blessing—not only because anyone could understand the songs but also because the kind of words he used helped the directors shoot the songs. His words inspired visuals that we could find around us, and we chose locations to shoot the songs according to some words that he had used in those songs. His lyrics would tell directors how to direct the songs, where to shoot them and how to make the characters behave in a certain way. That was the best thing about his writing. His knowledge went far beyond the words he used; he used everyday, normal, regular, conversational words and language, and that was the most beautiful thing about his writing.

The last word in songwriting is his lyrics from our film *Piya Ka Ghar*: '*Yeh jeevan hai, iss jeevan ka, yahi hai yahi hai, yahi hai rang roop, thode ghum hain, thodi khusiyan, yahi hai, yahi hai yahi hai chaaon dhoop.*'

He was very quick and prolific. He has written songs for our films, and even for films like *Milan* and *Jeene Ki Raah*, in front of me within twenty or thirty minutes. He never found it a problem and would write there and then. He would write as soon as he heard the tune, and he would write words that caught every note he'd heard in the tune, never missing a note, so sharp and well he wrote. He would use words that the character could sing, and never used words to impress others with his knowledge of Urdu or Hindi. He wrote for the characters according to their geographical location, circumstances and status. Like in the film *Milan*, he used the word *purwaiya* in his song 'Saawan Ka Mahina', and did not use the word *hawa*, because a boatman would use the word purwaiya for the wind that sails his boat. So deep was his understanding of the milieu he wrote for.

I was present during the sittings for all the songs he wrote for us and for the many films of Prasad Productions. The writing was so good that even after forty-eight years I can remember the main verses of all his songs. His verses have a very long life. In the song from *Raja Aur Runk*, 'Oh phirki waali, tu kal phir aana, nahin phir jaana,' he has used the word *phir* in three contexts. The first phir is on 'phirki waali'; the second phir means 'again'; and the third, phir jaana, means 'don't go back on your promise'. Such a play of words, with one word, three meanings! Such a talented writer! In the song *'Yeh dil deewana hai, dil toh deewana hai, deewana dil hai yeh, dil deeewana'*, he has used the words 'dil' and 'deewana' seven times in one verse, because the director wanted a song with the words repeated multiple times.

A.R. Rahman

Simple things are things that are very charming. Immediately charming to our senses. Because in a world of clutter and noise, simple things pop out; they create an impact immediately. Bakshiji was a king of that simplicity, I felt while working with him. He was very profound, yet how simple were his lyrics! That is actually an aspect of being a genius, I would say. Because only a genius can keep all the human complexities within and yet pull out an expression that is so simple, so charming, so easily.

An example of such genius in simplicity would be our song from *Taal* (1999): *'Kariye na, koi vada kissise kariye na, kariye toh vaada phir todiye na'*, and *'Nahin saamne yeh alag baat hai, mere pass hai tu mere paas hai'*. 'Kariye Na' was adapted for Andrew Lloyd Webber's theatre production; it's my favourite too.

Bakshiji had a good sense of music, and he had a good voice, so he would start singing his lyrics in his own tune! And what he sang would sound good too. So, I used to get a little 'tension' working with him, that if I delay making the tune for his lyrics, he may sing a better tune than I could make and then my director, Subhashji, would okay it. What am I doing there as the music composer? Music composers are expected to deliver hits. So it helps us if our lyrics writer has the ability to write a catchy and interesting mukhda. With Bakshi Sa'ab that was never a problem. Everything he wrote was so simple and attractive and phonetically interesting too. Honestly, I did not have to work hard at it. If you take the song 'Choli Ke Peeche', the sound of it is so musical and catchy, even if you don't know the meaning of the lyrics! Same for the rhyme of the song 'Taal Se Taal Mila'. People like him are blessed that they can give so much of themselves to their work, to their listeners.

Milan Luthria

The major decisions of your life can possibly make you or destroy you. But don't think too much before taking them; take them right away because the result of those decisions is not in your hands. However, for minor decisions, like, should I shave today or not, what should I have for dinner tonight, take a day or a week, because the results of such decision-making don't impact your life in any significant way.

When I was making *Kacche Dhaage*, on the very first song sitting, someone objected to Bakshiji using Punjabi words in the mukhda, '*Khali dil nai, jaan bhi yeh mangda, ishq di galli wich koi koi langda.*' He requested Bakshiji to write in Hindi even though I, the director, disagreed with him.

Bakshiji tried to explain to the producer, but he refused to budge. So Bakshiji asked me to come out of the room alone; he wanted to say something in private. Bakshiji said to me, and this is something I will never forget, 'This is the moment in your life, when you have two choices in front of you. Either you be a *ghulam* and listen to what people have to say to you against your beliefs, or you go with your conviction and become a film-maker. Ghulam or film-maker/director, today you make that decision.' We went in together and I insisted that we keep the Punjabi verse. That day I became a film-maker. The song was a hit and easily understood by listeners.

Tanuja Chandra

Bakshi Sa'ab came across as a quiet sort of man. I am sure with his friends and family he might have been talkative, but, for instance, if I were to ask him, 'Bakshi Sa'ab, *aap apne baare mein kuch bataiye,*' he possibly would have said, '*Bataane ke liye kya hai?*' even though he had lived such an eventful, varied life. He wasn't shy as a songwriter, though. His lyrics keenly illustrated his thoughts, his world view and, indeed, the expansive stature of his heart. His songs said so much about him.

When I narrated the story of *Dushman* to him, he listened quietly and merely said that it was a very difficult film to write songs for, and that he would need a couple days to think about it. With all the insecurity of a first-time director, I thought he didn't like the story and was indirectly turning the project down. How could a stalwart like him find it tough to write lyrics for any story, I thought. He couldn't possibly lack confidence, so maybe he was trying to say no politely. I was depressed. The next day he called me and asked me to come over. When we met, he recited the mukhda, '*Chitthi na koi sandesh, jaane woh kaun sa desh, jahan tum chale gaye.*' He said, 'This song will come when her sister dies. I feel now I can do justice to your film. I will write the songs for your film.'

Gulzar

Bakshi Sa'ab ke baare mein, ek toh yeh hai ki jis aadmi ne iss daur mein Hindi ke gaane radio pe sune aur agar woh Anand Bakshi ko naa jaanta ho, toh mera khayal hai woh Hindi cinema se naavaakif hai. He is such an essential name of our songs of Hindi films that he cannot be missed. Therefore, Bakshi Sa'ab is a complete era of Hindi film music. *Agar aap bahot pehle chale jayein, toh* writer D.N. Madhok *ya* Kedar Sharma, *unke naam aaye; lekin yeh jo pichla daur tha, beesvi sadi ki aakhri ki taraf,* from the time that Anand Bakshi came in, in the 1960s *woh sadi ke aakhir tak* Anand Bakshi *hi the. Yeh nahi ho sakta ki aap* Vividh Bharati radio *ka* programme *sunne aur usmein* Anand Bakshi *ya* Lata Mangeshkar *ka zikr na ho.* These two are the kinds of legends that are associated with the landmarks, milestones of Hindi film songs, and this is what Anand Bakshi is all about.

Bakshiji was a shayar. *Khush mijaaz aur khush dil bhi. Hamare yahan Urdu shayar ki* image *aisi thi ki daadi badi aur pyajama sambhaale hue bechara shayar keechad se guzar raha hai, kuch aisi* image *thi kuch logon ke dimaag mein. Lekin* Bakshi Sa'ab was not like that. This man was from services, Indian military. *Ek fauji ki jo dildaari hoti hai woh poori dildaari Bakshiji ki shaksiyat aur gaano mein nazar aati hai.*

Unki likhai . . . Phalsafe ko unhone phalsafe ki tarah kabhi nahi kaha. What he believed in, he believed in; but he never tried to define it, *aur koi* definition *banane ki koshish nahi ki,* neither did he ever intellectualize it. *Phalsafa* means philosophy. *Jawaan dil aur khush dil aur ussi tarah haske baat ki aur badi se badi baat ki. Unka gaana* 'Chingari koi bhadke, toh saawan usse bujhaaye, saawan jo aag lagaye, usse kaun bujhae.' This is totally a personal reaction, but according to me, *Amar Prem* was a great album of his. Then, Punjabi folk was on his lips and *gaate bhi bahot acha the woh, aur sur mein the.* Lataji *ke saath gaana bhi gaaya hai.* This is what Anand Bakshi is. Anand Bakshi *ko ek lafz mein* define *karna ho toh main sirf kahunga,* 'Cheers!'

Bakshiji did not consider his songwriting and did not take it up as a poet or intellectual. His career was about being a lyricist because his focus was on films. *Lekin yeh nahi ki woh shayar nahi the. Bilkul ek shayar the.* Urdu magazines *mein chappe hai unki nazmein, maine padhi hain.* He did not take up poetry as a profession, but writing songs is also a part of poetry. His focus was that he wanted to be a songwriter and lyricist of film songs. And that is why he was the most successful one out there.

Sameer Anjaan

Uss mukkamal fankar ke naam chand alfaaz jise main apana murshid maanata hoon . . .

Roohani mahake huve woh, khayalat kahan se laayen, lufz toh dhoondh len, lekin woh jazbaat kahaan se laayen, jo apane fun ke jadu se subko hasaata aur roolata hai, aisa Kalam ka jadugar, duniya me buss ek baar aata hai . . .

Irshad Kamil

My three favourite songs of Bakshiji are:

'Kuch Toh Log Kahenge' *sirf ek geet ke bol hi nahin hain balki chaar shabdon me bayan hamare samaaj ka bahut bada aur bahut zaroori sach hai. Anand Bakshi Sahab ke gaanon ki yahi khasiyat rahti hai. Wo apne gaanon me mithas barkarar rakhte hue samaaj ka bade se bada sach kah jaate hain. Amar Prem* film *ka yeh gana apne sach ki wazah se amar hua hai aur gaane me aaye aitihasik hawaale ki 'Sita bhi yahan badnaam hui' iss kadwe sach ko aur jyada majbooti dete hain. Ye geet mujhe Sahir Sahab ki bhi yaad dilata hai. Wo 'Jinhen Naaz Hai Hind Par Wo Kahan Hain' mein likhte hain, 'Yahan peer bhi aa chuke hain, jawan bhi, tan-o-mand bete bhi abba miyan bhi.' Usi darje par jakar Bakshi sahab likhte hain, 'Humko jo taane dete hain, hum khoye hain in rangraliyon me, humne unko bhi chhup chhup ke, aate dekhaa in galiyon me.'*

'Kuch Toh Log Kahenge' *geet kabhi purana nahin ho sakta.*

'Gadi Bula Rahi Hai' *seedhe aur saral tareeke se gadi ki nahin balki zindagi ki baat hai. Yahan bhi Bakshi Sahab ne behad bada phalsafa char asaan lafzon me kah diya hai aur wo hai, 'Chalna hi zindagi hai.'*

Mushkil vichar ko asaan banana aur asaan baat ko aam logon ki zuban par chadha dena ek hunar hai jo azeemkad geetkaar Bakshi Sahab *ke takreeban har geet me hai. Iss geet me unhone khel khel me kah diya, 'Seekho sabak jawanon.' Main is baat ko* 'Ekla Chalo Re' *ke baraks rakh ke bhi dekhta hun. Balki isme to sirf 'chalna' hai aur chhoti lekin aur bhi badi baat.*

'Yahan Main Ajnabi Hun' Bakshi Sahab *ka likha mera pasandeeda gana hai. Jis khoobsoorti se unhone is gaane me do vargon aur do samaajon ka zikr kiya hai wo sab itna asaan nahi tha jitna is gaane me lagta hai. Bhartiye aur pashchimi sabhyata ke beech ki kheencha taani, nimna–madhya warg aur uchcha warg ke beech ki khayin, masoomiyat aur chalaaki ke beech ka antar, kya nahi hai is gaane me! Aur in sabke sath mohabbat me adhikar ki baat,* 'Teri baahon me dekhun sanam gairon ki baahen, main launga kahan se bhala aisi nigahen?' *Shikwa, shikayat aur gile ki baat! Sirf yahi gaana nahin balki* Jab Jab Phool Khile *ke sab gaane hi taraashe hue nageene hain.*

Amitabh Bhattacharya

Bachpan se Bakshi Sahab *ke likhe gaane zubaani yaad hain. Kyunki wo sunane aur gaane me hamesha asaan lage. Lekin jab unke jaisa likhne ki nakaam koshish ki tab pata chala ki kitna mushkil kaam asaani se kar gaye* Bakshi Sahab. I salute the legend Anand Bakshi!

Manoj Muntashir

The magic of writing lies in its power to connect. Bakshi Sahab had mastered the art of connecting to the listeners very subtly, on a very subconscious level. That's what turned many of his songs into idioms and proverbs. One such song is 'Yahan Main Ajnabi Hoon'. No matter how socially active or accepted we are, at some point in time we feel as if we are living in an alien world. In my case, this is a very regular phenomenon. Every now and then I go through this *bairag*, the strong desire to escape from everything good and bad around me as I just don't relate to any of it. When it happens, the only song I take refuge in is 'Yahan Main Ajnabi Hoon'. This haunted feeling of being in a strange world became all the more agonizing when I moved to Mumbai from my small town Gaurigunj in Uttar Pradesh. I could not get accustomed to a city which has no breaks in its system, only accelerators. Nobody has time for anyone. Back in Gaurigunj, everyone knew everyone; in Mumbai, people living in the same building are clueless about each other. I remember playing the following verses in loop while staying in an Andheri hutment: '*Kahan shamo-sahar ye, kahan din-raat mere* . . . *Bahut ruswa hue hain yahan jazbaat mere. Nayi tahzeeb hai ye, naya hai ye zamana* . . . *Magar main aadmi hoon, wahi sadiyon purana.*'

In a society like India, where we have 5000 years of imposed moral values and so-called *sanskars* to carry on our shoulders, Bakshi Sahab had the creative courage to rebel against all of it. In one plain and simple line, he burst the bubble of pretentious social dynamics: '*Kuch toh log kahenge logon ka kaam hai kehna.*' If I am asked to pick the top ten all-time greatest songs of India, this one may just find its place on the topmost spot. '*Kuch reet jagat ki aisi hai, har ek subah ki shaam hui* . . . *Tu kaun hai, tera naam hai kya? Sita bhi yahan badnaam hui.*' Anyone who has heard and mulled over this song even once will stop caring for the world with immediate effect. Also, this song is a brilliant example of cinematic writing. Fifty scenes in the film *Amar Prem* would not have been as effective in describing Rajesh Khanna's character as the few words of this song were. Another example of Bakshi Sahab being the best screen lyricist of all time is the film *Darr*. Shah Rukh's character was very complex and layered for the time of the film's release. I can bet that the audience would have never understood the plot of the film, nor adjusted to the anti-hero philosophy of Yash Chopraji, in the absence of the song 'Tu Hai Meri Kiran'. Look at these nine simple words which magically encapsulate the 150 pages of the script, '*Tu haan kar ya na kar, tu hai meri kiran.*'

I remember writing songs for *Badshaho*, which was being directed by Milan Luthria. Every time we sat to make a song, he would sigh and say that he was missing Bakshi Sahab. In fact, it was one of the most challenging films of my career, as I was writing for a director whose taste buds were used to the legendary Bakshi Sahab's words. India is a land of poets and writers. Many more will come, but Bakshi Sahab will always be missed with the same sigh, forever.

Vijay Akela*

Anand Bakhshi is the Mir Taqi Mir, Nazeer Akbarabadi and Kabir Das of modern times. *Yun toh sabne geet likhe, sab mein hi auqat thi, Bakhshi mein ek baat hai aur Bakhshi mein ek baat thi.*

---

* Vijay Akela was the first to publish a book on Anand Bakshi, a compilation of his best and hit songs, *Main Shayar Badnaam*, published in Hindi by Rajkamal Prakashan.

Epilogue

When Anand Bakshi turned sixty-eight (1998), his friend and *Indian Express* journalist Ali Peter John had a conversation with him. What follows is excerpted from that poignant and pertinent exchange they had as professionals and close friends.

* * *

'Main Waqt Ka Mureed Hoon'

I was, I remain, just an ordinary man, floating in the tide of time, trying my best to keep up with time, and to keep up with the times. Trying to run ahead, sometimes only in my imagination. It's fun trying to run ahead of time in your imagination. But it will not be possible for any man, however intelligent he may become in the next three trillion years and more, to catch up with time. Time, that elusive colourful bird no human can challenge, whatever progress he has made or will make.

Why am I talking about time? Well, there are many reasons. Let us go over them one by one.

Today, on this New Year's Day, the world has lived for 1998 years, according to the 'calendar of time' made by man. Time has gone by for all of us. As for me, I have seen time flying. Faster than I

Laxmikant, Jamuna, Tarachand Barjatya, Vasantrao Naik (chief minister of Maharashtra), Anand Bakhshi and Nutan at the golden jubilee celebration of *Milan*, 1967

At the first house he owned, Raj Pipla, in Santacruz West, Linking Road, Mumbai

NUMBER ONE!

Laxmikant, Anand Bakhshi and Pyarelal; a news feature
captioning the trio as 'Number One', 1970s

With R.D. Burman, working on the song 'Dum Maro Dum' from *Hare Rama Hare Krishna*, 1970s

Recordist O.D. Bhansali, Mohan Kumar, Pyarelal, Laxmikant and Anand Bakhshi at the recording of Bakhshi's first song as singer, for *Mome Ki Gudiya*, at Famous Studios, 10 December 1971

Dharmendra, Sapan Chakraborty, Dulal Guha, Anand Bakhshi and R.D. Burman celebrating the success of *Dost*, 1974

The Bakshi family with Ustaad Chittar Mal (in spectacles) and Dr Nanavati,
Secunderabad, 1976

With his firstborn and good-luck charm, Suman, at her wedding, 15 May 1977

With Amitabh Bachchan and Yash Johar in Ooty, shooting for the song 'Dillagi Ne Di Hawa', from the movie *Dostana*, 1979

Bakhshi taking part in the 'walk or dance with a whisky glass balanced on your head' challenge with family and friends, 1980s

With Subhash Ghai, a friend who always stood by him and his family, at the launch of *Taal*, 25 January 1998

Nusrat Fateh Ali Khan listening to Anand Bakhshi sing at his daughter Kavita Sanjiv Bali's house, New Delhi, 1990s

I am a being of Divine light
And Power - I have -
Access to all that the universe
Offer - I can Reach out
And Take or do whatever
I want - whenever I want -

Bakhshi began every '*gaane ki kitaab*' with this affirmation; a snapshot of a page from his last song diary, 2001

Bakhshi writing lyrics on the eve of his sixty-eighth birthday, picture by Mukta Arts Limited, 1998

Our prayer room had a hand-knitted wall hanging that said, 'A family that prays together stays together'

Our last photo with the pillar of our family, our mother, Kamla Bakhshi, with her sons-in-law Vinay Datt and Sanjiv Bali, at her daughter Suman's house, 19 June 2008

could see. I have tried my best to understand time and why it flies, and flies so fast that no man or superman, no supersonic jet, not even the greatest progress made by man who is always in the mood to challenge even the gods by playing some petty and clever games, has succeeded in catching it, arresting it. Forget catching, even feeling what it would be like to catch up with time. Let all the great scientists, engineers and cosmonauts, and those who dare to challenge the power of time, try and keep trying. But I dare not try.

I don't know how many trillion years have passed by us, but the fact is that a lot of time has passed by. It has never stopped for any power, any emperor, any culture, any civilization.

Perhaps time is as more elusive than God. Or perhaps, time is God. Time and God talk best to us when we are alone.

I am also thinking so much about time because I am surprised that I have (somehow) lived for sixty-eight long years! I have faced all kinds of ups and downs. In my family, my health and at work. I am no exception; everyone is carrying a cross. Because I have had some health issues in the last two decades, though they did not stop me from ploughing ahead and doing my best, I feel I have lived longer than I should have. Yes, I should have died by now, I think. But then, time, yes, that elusive bird, I think, has a plan for me too; in fact, it has a design for every man and woman. A design that is never revealed, and everyone has to unravel their own designs tailor-made for them by the master artist—time. *Waqt*. According to time's designs, it's evident to me, only now at sixty-eight, that I have still some time to go to that great 'beyond' where time will, finally, not matter. A place where I will become 'one' with time.

I must say, admit, that time has been extremely kind to me. Benevolent, in fact. That's why I am philosophical about time today, at sixty-eight, and I feel extremely grateful to time for giving me the time to thank 'time'. I must confess, I have enjoyed every moment of the time that I've been gifted with—time with my family, my listeners, people I worked with, people I worked for, people I never even met but heard through my subconscious self-expressions, those from my world and those beyond my own little world. I've been given so much, so many blessings and gifts, that I will have absolutely no regrets if time takes me away whenever 'it is time' according to time's beautiful, mysterious and discreet designs and plans.

Just pause and think for just a moment, about my relationship with time. I was a young man when I fell in love with poetry. With singing and making up 'dhuns' for my poetry. Poetry become my passion, yet writing did not have the power to give me my next meal. I had joined the Royal Indian Navy before Partition. The kind English commanding officer, A.C. Moore, who had 'caught' me taking part in the naval mutiny of 1944 at the Karachi port, said to me, out of pity, 'You are just a boy, too young to go to jail, and if I put you in jail, which I can, your life would mostly be ruined forever. So I will dismiss you from the service without arresting you on the charge of indulging with your mates against the British Empire.'

Post Partition, I joined the Indian Army. We were living as refugees, with my family scattered across Delhi and Lucknow. I joined as an ordinary sepoy. God knows I could have fallen to an enemy's bullet while I was there, as I got posted in the infantry division later, but nothing like that happened. I let time take its own decisions for me.

Time took its decision for me. I quit the army and came to Mumbai, where I was told poetry had some chance of surviving because of the film industry. Poetry and, naturally, the poet. I never ever considered myself a great poet, just a songwriter for films, but the outpourings of my heart, which I spilled on paper, were called poetry by my friends, and well-wishers told me that I was a poet too. I did not want to believe them. I tried peddling my poems, trying to find admirers, for my encouragement, and buyers for the poems, so I could feed myself and my family. During Partition, we had left a palatial house and had become refugees overnight. We had a large joint family to feed and shelter.

When I was in the Indian Army, from 1947 to 1956, I never knew that you could make a living from your words, your thoughts, your innermost feelings. Bombay, and especially the film industry, made me realize, by the late '60s, that my kind of songwriting, or poetry, stood a very good chance. I knew I was no Mirza Ghalib or Mir or Sahir Ludhianvi or even a Rajendra Krishan, but I had some friends, like my mentor poet Bismil Saeedi, later my ticket collector friend, Ustaad Chhitar Mal Swaroop, and my army mates and seniors, who had said that I had all the makings of a complete lyricist. I knew a poet who wrote songs for films according to situations created by writers, directors and producers, and sometimes by illiterate financiers and distributors who didn't know what this madness called poetry was but always said, *'Film mein kuch achcha gaana vaana ho jaana chaahiye, nahin to kya mazaa hai film banane mein* (A film should have a few nice songs, otherwise what's the fun in film-making).' Songs were very important to these people and to people in general. As important as they were to me when I was still a child. Time brought songs to me right from the time I was a child. I remember my mother, Mitra (Sumitra), singing to me. She passed away when I was five or six, but her songs have always remained with me. The mother–child songs I wrote were from my memories of her.

Time was first very kind to me when I got the biggest film of my life. Even though it did not work at the box office, it was my FIRST film: *Bhala Admi*, by a bhala aadmi, the star actor Bhagwan Dada. Time was then most kind to me when I got an opportunity to write all the songs for another film, *Jab Jab Phool Khile*. The success of our songs across India made 'Anand Bakshi' *ek bikne waali cheez* (a saleable commodity) overnight! However, my songs were for sale, not me, and this attitude I think brought respect my way too. *Jab Jab Phool Khile* opened the pearly gates of a whole new world of my dreams to me. For the first time I was able to provide well for my family—my primary mission—whom I had felt I had let down for more than a decade with my passion to make it in films but without any money in my pockets. Soon, more and more producers and directors came to me, particularly after *Milan*; *Milan ne meri taqdeer ke darwaze khol diye* (*Milan* opened the doors of my destiny).

Subsequently, *Farz, Aradhana, Do Raste* became back-to-back superhits, within a span of less than five years. I have never lacked good work and money since, by the grace of God alone. So, you see, waqt has been very kind to me. Even today, at sixty-eight, I am writing romantic songs for teenagers for the industry's topmost directors, producers and actors. From a matriculate soldier earning Rs 75 a month, to a refugee, no house, living at railway station waiting rooms for three years, to someone who has two houses today, I have been a recipient of time's kindness. They want me to write the songs for all their films, big and small, social and thrillers, any genre, for all age groups, all religions.

They feel I can do it, so I go with it. What more did I want? I was just looking for another chance to write more songs, and success simply followed my efforts. I did not work for success. I began just to secure my family and my firstborn, *meri beti*, Pappi; Gogi, my second-born; and Kamla, my pillar.

Even back then, I knew that I could write songs for any occasion. But my confidence was just to show to other people. Deep inside, I secretly felt nervous before writing any song. I just never told anyone. I have suffered from a feeling of helplessness since my teens. More so after I gained success in the late '60s. I somehow kept growing more and more successful and popular as a lyricist. I felt hurt that they called me a fluke, but I never spoke against them. I just said what I always felt—that I am not a poet, I am just a songwriter. And I decided firmly that I would never show off my talent or success, because something within me told me that the day I misuse the gift that was granted to me by God and time, I would be nowhere very soon. I would be finished! Never abuse a blessing or gift. Be humble, '*Kyunki, humne dekhe hain bade bade, gir jaate hain khade khade.*' I have read about, and even seen, the most formidable and talented people fail overnight—

because of an unhealthy attitude towards their work and their success. Because they did not respect what time brought to their threshold.

Immediately upon my success, I realized that time, in particular, was very kind to me. Even success was kind to me. I was writing songs for all those composers, actors, producers, singers and music directors whose names I had heard when I was a schoolboy, then a navy cadet and subsequently a sepoy, a soldier. I was so low in rank, if I were to retire from the army with my matriculation qualification, I would have perhaps retired as a subedar. There was a flood of opportunities and I didn't let any of them go. I knew there was money in what I was doing, but I knew that there was something more than money that mattered—I wanted to be taken seriously as a lyricist; I didn't want to be called a 'wordsmith'. I wanted to be someone whose words, however simple, touched the heart of every man, woman and child. And by God's grace, and time's, my pen and I succeeded. Thanks to so many directors, composers, singers, story writers, and to luck and waqt, for teaming up with me.

I was on top, along with some others, in the late '60s, '70s, '80s, '90s. Did I say '90s? Yes, I have reached the '90s, and I just don't know how. *Dilwale Dulhania Le Jayenge* and *Dil Toh Pagal Hai* are very big musical hits. There has been so much competition all along! Such good lyricists have been writing since the time I first arrived here with my pen and diary. There have been so many better lyricists than me. There have been so many good poets who have tried to be lyricists, some only because of the money, which is a necessity, and I needed it for my family's security. They deserved to be far bigger than me as writers. Why they could not be so was maybe because luck and waqt, *dono hi unke saath nahi the* (both were against them).

There are also many younger lyricists today who are making more money than good poetry. I've purposely made that statement because today is really the time of the lyricists. There are so many songs, all kinds of songs and films are being made, and these songs have lyricists, and all kinds of lyricists. The man who writes film songs, whether it is poetry or not, has to write songs that appeal to people across India, people who have no time to look at dictionaries to find out the meanings of the words in the songs. Write using simple words if you are a film lyricist, unless the story demands words that are not commonly used by most people in their daily conversations.

I, Anand Prakash Bakhshi, Nand, have written all kinds of songs. Like I always say, a lyricist has to be able to write a song for any moment the screenplay demands. However, I have not catered to the basic raw instincts of man, the instincts that cannot be discussed at the family table. Never. I may have written naughty songs, mischievous songs, but at sixty-eight I don't think I will stoop to write songs that cannot be heard by the entire family. My own children are my barometer.

I feel very happy when a very young Aditya Chopra or a Tanuja Chandra comes to me and asks me to write their songs. I don't know them. I don't know how their mind works and what kind of films they are planning. But there is something about these new film-makers. They are very clear about what they want, and they see to it that they get what they want from a senior writer like me. They respect Anand Bakshi, the name, but when it comes to work, they want Anand Bakshi to come up with his best, and age does not matter in this profession. Talent, discipline, punctuality, hard work, purity of heart matter. They suggest changes, and I have to make changes because this is their generation. We 'older' writers must listen to them, or else no one will listen to us. Simple. *Waqt ke saath chalna zaroori hai. Issi liye, main waqt ka mureed hoon* and I always respected whatever time brought to my door, right from the time I left the army to now.

There is one thing for which I shall always be grateful to the great Sahir Ludhianvi and scriptwriters Salim–Javed. Sahir Sahab always said that he would take one rupee more than what was charged by the music director. He taught us self-worth, that we writers must be proud of our contribution to a film and should not consider ourselves any less than those we work as a team with. I thank Salim–Javed because writers like them made stars out of us lyricists and poets by giving us, as well as directors, great and inspiring screenplays. They proved with their rightful pride in their efforts, success and attitude that if your work is good, you can ask for the money you deserve, and if you stand up for yourself, your craft and talent, producers, the world, will give it to you.

According to one survey, I have written about 4000 songs in thirty-odd years. I am not sure. But I continue to feel blessed that I am still writing! Many of them are songs for youngsters.

However, I will write only till time wants me to. *Mera aur waqt ka janam janam ka sath hai. Main waqt ka mureed hoon. Is duniya se uss duniya mein jaane tak, waqt aur mera saath rahega. Aur wahan, main pariyon ke liye geet likhoonga, zaroor likhoonga. Kyunki, geet likhna mera janam janam ka dharma hai. Insaano ke liye nahi toh pariyon aur farishton ke liye hi sahi, mere dharma aur karma, agar waqt mera saath wahan bhi de jahaan woh mujhe le chalega iss duniya ke paar.*

Anand Prakash Bakhshi

What's a Legend?

We use the term 'legend' for people who are always remembered fondly and whose work survives for decades. There is one more meaning to this term that I learnt from a humble flute seller.

A few years ago, I heard a young flute seller playing 'Mere Naina Sawan Bhado . . .' from the film *Mehbooba*. He was walking by the street right below my house. I called out to him and asked him to come up to the second floor.

I told him he was a wonderful player and that I wanted to reward him. I gifted him Rs 50. He accepted the money and was surprised that I did not want to buy a flute in return. I noticed that he had no slippers on.

He insisted I take a flute, and so I did, in return for what I had given him. He was a man of pride in his trade. Truly earning his livelihood. I asked him if he knew the name of the lyricist, music composer and singer whose song he was playing on the street to sell his flutes. He replied that he didn't.

I asked him to come in and led him to our living room, where a lot of Dad's trophies and awards have been put on display. I opened an album of Dad's work colleagues and began to show him photos of Dad, R.D. Burman and many other 'legends'. He admitted that he had neither heard of them nor seen their photos but had picked up the dhun from the radio.

He would touch every photograph I showed him and then touch his heart, as though he was seeking their blessings. I was moved by his gesture. I asked him why he was doing that. He replied, 'Sa'ab, *inn logon ki wajeh se hum teen waqt ki roti khaate hain* (It's because of these people that I get three square meals).'

My Favourites

Let me reiterate here, that we need to publish more than one volume on Anand Bakshi to try and do justice to his story and the songs he co-created with his composers, singers, directors, actors, musicians . . . To get a better sense of his work, you may watch some of the films I've listed below and listen to the songs. This is just a selection of my favourites from the nearly 630-plus films he wrote lyrics for. Why do I suggest you watch these films? Because a lyricist's work is best appreciated in the context of the film's story.

1959

Bhala Admi, C.I.D. Girl, Ek Armaan Mera, Lal Nishan, Maine Jeena Seekh Liya

1960s

Mehlon Ke Khwab, Jasoos, Zameen Ke Taare, Razia Sultana, Warrant, Banke Sanwaria, Aaye Din Bahaar Ke, Kala Samunder, Jab Se Tumhen Dekha Hai, Phool Bane Angaare, Mr. X in Bombay, Himalay Ki God Mein, Teesra Kaun, Aasra, Chhota Bhai, Devar, Aamne Saamne, Chandan Ka Palna, Night in London, Taqdeer, Raja Aur Runk, Anjaana, Aya Sawan Jhoom Ke, Jeene Ki Raah, Jigri Dost, Mahal, Sajan, Mehndi Lagi Mere Haath, Jab Jab Phool Khile, Milan, Farz, Aradhana, Do Raaste

1970s

Aan Milo Sajna, Geet, Ishq Par Zor Nahin, Jeevan Mrityu, Kati Patang, Amar Prem, Khilona, My Love, Mere Humsafar, Sharafat, The Train, Aap Aye Bahaar Ayee, Dushman, Haathi Mere Saathi, Hare Rama Hare Krishna, Main Sunder Hoon, Maryada, Mehboob Ki Mehndi, Mera Gaon Mera Desh, Naya Zamana, Paraya Dhan, Uphaar, Anuraag, Apna Desh, Mome Ki Gudiya, Jawani Diwani, Raja Jani, Seeta Aur Geeta, Zindagi Zindagi, Bobby, Heera Panna, Jheel Ke Us Paar, Jugnu, Kuchhe Dhaage, Loafer, Namak Haraam, Raja Rani, Manchali, Shareef Budmaash, Aap Ki Kasam, Ajnabee, Dost, Majboor, Prem Nagar, Roti, Chupke Chupke, Julie, Pratiggya, Prem Kahani, Sholay, Aap Beati, Balika Badhu, Barood, Bairaag, Charas, Maha Chor, Mehbooba, Amar Akbar Anthony, Anurodh, Apnapan, Dharam Veer, Dream Girl, Mukti, Yehi Hai Zindagi, Aahutee, Satyam Shivam Sundaram, Azaad, Dil Aur Deewar, Main Tulsi Tere Aangan Ki, Pati Patni Aur Woh, Shalimar, Gautam Govinda, Jurmana, Kali Ghata, Mr Natwarlal, Sargam, Suhaag, The Great Gambler

1980s

Aap Ke Deewane, Aasha, Aas Paas, Abdullah, Dostana, Hum Paanch, Judaai, Karz, Patita, Shaan, Ek Duje Ke Liye, Love Story, Naseeb, Rocky, Bemisaal, Desh Premee, Ghazab, Rajput, Shakti, Teri Kasam, Vidhaata, Andhaa Kaanoon, Arpan, Avtaar, Betaab, Coolie, Hero, Lovers, Nastik, Woh 7 Din, Zara Si Zindagi, Sohni Mahiwal, Aar Paar, Meri Jung, Yudh, Amrit, Karma, Naam, Nagina, Sindoor, Shahenshah, Chaalbaaz, Chandni, Ram Lakhan, Tridev, Awaargi, Agneepath

1990s

Akayla, Pati Patni Aur Tawaif, Hum, Lamhe, Saudagar, Angaar, Heer Ranjha, Khuda Gawah, Kshatriya, Parampara, Vishwatma,

Darr, Gumraah, Khal Nayak, Sahibaan, Mohra, Dilwale Dulhania Le Jayenge, Ram Jaane, Trimurti, Dhun, Jaan, Rajkumar, Tere Mere Sapne, Ankhon Mein Tum Ho, Deewana Mastana, Dil Toh Pagal Hai, Ghulam-E-Mustafa, Gupt, Pardes, Dushman, Jab Pyaar Kisise Hota Hai, Zakhm, Aarzoo, Dil Kya Kare, Kachche Dhaage, Taal, Love You Hamesha

2000, 2001, 2002

Hadh Kar Di Aapne, Yeh Raaste Hain Pyaar Ke, Nayak, Pyaar Ishq Aur Mohabbat, Rahul, Raju Chacha, Mohabbatein, Gadar: Ek Prem Katha, Asoka (one song), *Yaadein, Mujhse Dosti Karoge, Kranti, Kitne Door Kitne Paas, Na Tum Jaano Na Hum, The Hero*

2012

Yeh Jo Mohabbat Hai (one song)
There are also a few unreleased songs, from released and unreleased films, I have made available on his YouTube channel for listeners, as they belong to you all.

* * *

I leave you dear readers with that which empowers me, a statement of my daddy's, which I recite as a prayer at night or early in the morning, whenever I feel overwhelmed by my situation or circumstance:

> There is something inside me superior to my circumstances and stronger than any situation in life.

Rakesh Anand Bakshi

Highlights of Anand Bakshi's Career
(1956–2002)

His association with music composers:

Three hundred three films with Laxmikant–Pyarelal (1680 songs)
Ninety-nine with R.D. Burman
Thirty-four with Kalyanji–Anandji
Twenty-six with Anu Malik
Fourteen with S.D. Burman
Thirteen with Rajesh Roshan
Ten with Viju Shah
Ten with Anand–Milind
Eight with Bappi Lahiri
Seven with Roshan
Seven with Jatin–Lalit
Seven with S. Mohinder (Mohinder Singh)
Seven with Uttam Singh
Seven with N. Datta (Datta Naik)
Five with Shiv–Hari
Four with Dilip Sen and Sameer Sen
Three with A.R. Rahman
Three with Ravindra Jain
Three with Usha Khanna

Three with S.D. Batish (Nirmal Kumar)
Three with Nikhil Kamath and Vinay Tiwari
Three with Anand Raj Anand
Two with Chitragupt
Two with C. Ramchandra
Two with Anil Biswas
Two with Sardul Qatra
Two with M.M. Kreem (M.M. Keeravani)
Two with Nadeem–Shravan
Two with Darshan Rathod and Sanjeev Rathod (Sanjeev–Darshan)
Two with Datta Ram (Dattaram Wadkar)
Two with Amar–Utpal
Two with Naushad
Two with Sajid–Wajid
Two with Surendra Singh Sodhi
One with Shankar–Jaikishan
One with Vishal Bhardwaj
One with Ismail Darbar
One with Rahul Sharma
One with Nusrat Fateh Ali Khan
One with Sukhwinder Singh
One with Salil Chowdhary
One with Nisar Bazmi
One with B.N. Bali
One with Ravi
One with Bulo C. Rani
One with Lachhiram
One with Vasant Desai
One with Raju Singh
One with G.S. Kohli
One with S.N. Tripathi
One with Dhansingh
One with Kishore Kumar

One with Sameer Phatarpekar
One with Sapan Chakraborty
One with Anjan Biswas
One with Neeraj Vora and Uttank Vora
One with Babloo Chakravorty
One with Agosh
One with Adnan Sami (incomplete/unreleased)
One with Amjad Ali Khan (incomplete/unreleased)

Geetmala Listeners' Verdict: 1967–2001

Here's a list of Anand Bakshi's songs over the years that topped the annual charts on India's most popular countdown show from 1967 to 2000, *Binaca Geetmala*, which became *Cibaca Geetmala* in 1986, *Cibaca Sangeetmala* in 1989 and *Colgate Cibaca Geetmala* in 2000:

1967

'Saawan Ka Mahina Pawan Kare Sor'
(Laxmikant–Pyarelal/Lata Mageshkar/Mukesh)
Film: *Milan*

1970

'Bindiya Chamkegi Chhoodi Khankegi'
(Laxmikant–Pyarelal/Lata)
Do Raaste

1972

'Dum Maro Dum'
(R.D. Burman/Asha Bhosle)
Hare Rama Hare Krishna

1980

'Dafli Wale Dafli Baja'
(Laxmikant–Pyarelal/Mohammed Rafi/Lata)
Sargam

1984

'Tu Mera Jaanu Hai Tu Mera Dilbar Hai'
(Laxmikant–Pyarelal /Manhar Udhaas/Anuradha Paudwal)
Hero

1987

'Chitthi Aai Hai'
(Laxmikant–Pyarelal/Pankaj Udhas)
Naam

1989

'My Name Is Lakhan'
(Laxmikant–Pyarelal/Mohammad Aziz)
Ram Lakhan

1993

'Choli Ke Peeche Kya Hai'
(Laxmikant–Pyarelal/Alka Yagnik/Ela Arun)
Khal Nayak

1995

'Tujhe Dekha Toh Yeh Jaana Sanam'
(Jatin–Lalit/Udit Narayan/Lata)
Dilwale Dulhania Le Jayenge

1999

'Taal Se Taal Mila'
(A.R. Rahman/Udit/Alka)
Taal

2000

'Humko Humi Se Chura Lo'
(Jatin–Lalit//Lata/Udit)
Mohabbatein

Out of the nearly 2094 songs that played on this weekly radio show, Anand Bakshi's songs played nearly 392 times from 1962 to 2006. There were a few years in between when this programme did not air.

Nominees/winners of Filmfare Awards

'Kora Kaagaz Tha Yeh Man Mera', *Aradhana*, 1970
'Aane Se Uske Aaye Bahaar', *Jeene Ki Raah*, 1970
'Bindiya Chamkegi Chhoodi Kankegi', *Do Raaste*, 1971
'Na Koi Umang Hai, Na Koi Tarang Hai', *Kati Patang*, 1972
'Chingari Koi Bhadke', *Amar Prem*, 1973
'Main Shayar Badnaam', *Namak Haram*, 1973
'Hum Tum Ek Kamre Mein Band Hon', *Bobby*, 1974
'Main Shayar Toh Nahin', *Bobby*, 1974
'Gaadi Bula Rahi Hai', *Dost*, 1975
'Aayegi Zaroor Chitthi, Mere Naam Ki', *Dulhan*, 1976
'Mehbooba O Mehbooba', *Sholay*, 1976
'Mere Naina Sawan Badho', *Mehbooba*, 1977
'Parda Hai Parda', *Amar Akbar Anthony*, 1978
'Main Tulsi Tere Aangan Ki', *Main Tulsi Tere Angan Ki*, 1979
'Aadmi Musafir Hai', *Apnapan*, 1979 (awarded)

'Sawan Ke Jhoole Padhe', *Jurmana*, 1980
'Dafli Wale Dafli Baja, *Sargam*, 1980
'Sheesha Ho Ya Dil Ho', *Aasha*, 1981
'Om Shanti Om', *Karz*, 1981
'Dard-E-Dil, Dard-E-Jigar', *Karz*, 1981
'Bane Chahe Dushman Zamana Humara', *Dostana*, 1981
'Solah Baras Ki Bali Umar Ko Salaam', *Ek Duje Ke Liye*, 1982
'Tere Mere Beech Mein', *Ek Duje Ke Liye*, 1982 (awarded)
'Yaad Aa Rahi Hai', *Love Story*, 1982
'Jab Hum Jawaan Honge', *Betaab*, 1984
'Sohni Chanab De Kinare Pukare Tera Naam', *Sohni Mahiwal*, 1985
'Zindagi Har Qadam Ek Nayi Jang Hai', *Meri Jung*, 1987
'Lagi Aaj Sawan Ki Phir Woh Jhadi Hai', *Chandni*, 1990
'Choli Ke Peeche Kya Hai', *Khal Nayak*, 1993
'Jaadu Teri Nazar', *Darr*, 1994
'Tu Cheez Badi Hai Mast Mast', *Mohra*, 1995
'Ghar Aaja Pardesi Tera Des Bulaye Re', *Dilwale Dulhania Le Jayenge*, 1996
'Tujhe Dekha Toh Yeh Jana Sanam', *Dilwale Dulhania Le Jayenge*, 1996 (awarded)
'Bholi Si Surat Aankhon Mein Masti', *Dil Toh Pagal Hai*, 1998
'I Love My India', *Pardes*, 1998
'Zara Tasveer Se Tu Utar Ke Saamne Aa', *Pardes*, 1998
'Taal Se Taal Mila', *Taal*, 2000
'Ishq Bina Kya Jeena Yaaron', *Taal*, 2000 (awarded)
'Humko Humi Se Chura Lo', *Mohabbatein*, 2001
'Udja Kaale Kawan', *Gadar: Ek Prem Katha*, 2002
'Main Nikla Gaddi Le Ke', *Gadar: Ek Prem Katha*, 2002

The Relevance of Anand Bakshi Today

Vijay Akela (poet, lyricist, radio host)

Yun to sabne geet likhe
Sab hi me auqaat thi
Bakhshi me ek baat hai aur
Bakhshi me ek baat thi.

Bakhshi aaj bhi utne hi saamayik (contemporary) hain jitne bees saal pahle the. Jab wo hayaat the aur geet likh rahe the.

Woh apne geeton ko desi muhawaredaar boli ka pairahan dete the, jinme na sirf us daur ke balki har daur ke aakhiri sach ki parakh hoti thi. Mushkil lafzon ko unhone adab (literature) ki gahri sazish samjha aur isiliye hamesha asaan lafzon ko pahchaan kar apne geeton ki qismat sanwaara kiye.

Bakhshi ko samajhna ho to zara Mumbai ki sarhad se baahar nikal jaiye. Aap ko lagega ki aaj Anand Bakhshi kal se bhi zyada lokpriye aur aadarniye hain!

Geeton me chhupe Bakhshi ke shandaar khayalon ko apna khayal kahne wale directors kahan gaye aaj? Jo scriptwriters kahte the 'Agar hamare situations achchhe na hote toh Bakhshi itna achchha thode likhte.' Woh situations kahan ghark ho gaye aaj? Bakhshi ke jaate hi unke qile kyun dhwast ho gaye aaj?

Bakhshi ko samman dene se katrane wale hamare isi desh me aaj jab bhi koi aandolan hota hai, Karma *ka 'Dil diya hai jaan bhi denge ae watan tere liye' hi bajaya jaata hai. Aaj bhi birthday par* Farz *ka hi geet bajaya jaata hai: 'Baar baar din ye aaye, baar baar dil yeh gaye.'*

'Chitthi na koi sandes/jaane wo kaun sa des/jahan tum chale gaye', jo aaj bhi sabse zyada bajne wale geeton me ek hai, Jagjit Singh *ka nahi,* Anand Bakhshi *ka likha geet hai.*

Hindostan ki do sabse jyada chalne wali filmein Sholay *aur* Dilwale Dulhaniya Le Jayenge *(jo aaj bhi chal rahi hai)* Bakhshi *ke geeton se hi roshan hain na?*

Bakhshi ek chiragh the jinki style of writing *se na jaane kitne deeye jale. Maine swaym unse hi likhna seekha, aur jab gahre utra to paya ki* songs of Bakhshi and Bakhshi's style of writing *kuchh aur nahi balki dil-o-dimagh ko sukoon pahunchane wali ek shifa hai.*

Dr Rajiv M. Vijayakar (journalist, author, film historian)

Anand Bakshi continues to be relevant. Every year that quotient increases as we realize that he was no mere lyricist—he was a visionary and philosopher without peer, who lived very much in the present. His thoughts and his pen remained strongly contemporary, with a healthy futuristic quality and timelessness, despite working across five decades and with multiple generations of composers. That is why, even today's generation finds Anand Bakshi and his thoughts relevant (as will those not even born as yet). And that is the definition of a visionary.

Bakshi's mastery—in songs like 'Gaadi Bula Rahi Hai', 'Chitthi Aayi Hai', 'Pardesiyon Se Na Ankhiyaan Milana', 'Chingari Koi Bhadke', 'Dil Kya Kare Jab Kisiko', 'Ghar Aaja Pardesi', 'Roop Tera Mastana'—was unparalleled. 'Story *sunkar hi* mind *chalta hai!*' was his memorable quote to me. But, as composer Ismail Darbar once said, 'Baap re! *Kya cheez hai* Bakshi Sa'ab!'

The reason was that Bakshi never gave just two or three antaras as per the needs of the song. He would offer—for each of the 6000 songs he wrote!—a minimum eight to ten, from which he would tell his associates to choose. Look at the wealth we have all missed—we have heard only 20 per cent of Bakshi's actual output!

Needless to say, *all* the antaras he wrote were relevant to the situation and many even helped shape the song's picturization, if not the film's script! A perfect example was the title song of the superhit South potboiler *Swarag Se Sunder*, in which he wrote the line '*Apna ghar hai swarag se sunder*' for the hero. The heroine retorts, '*Swarag mein kahaan se aaye macchar?*' And the hero replies, '*Arey macchar bhi aashiq hain tere, kya karoon!*'

Perceptive to the core, he once told me that over the last few years, the sad song had almost disappeared, with this simple truth as explanation for the way film music was going: 'Because you can't dance while singing a sad song!' He paused and, with a mischievous glint in his eye, added, 'Or maybe people are not sad any more!'

One reason why Bakshi was never outdated had to do with his firm belief that different eras see not only different talents but different trends. Having worked with composers all the way from the late '50s (when he began) to the turn of the century, he knew he had to work with generations far younger than him, and he never baulked at that. Rather, he enjoyed it.

In 2000, he signed a film with Himesh Reshammiya, which never took off. His success stories with Nadeem–Shravan, Jatin–Lalit, Shiv–Hari, Viju Shah, M.M. Kreem, A.R. Rahman, Dilip Sen–Sameer Sen, Sajid–Wajid, Nusrat Fateh Ali Khan and even Neeraj–Uttank are well known. Ditto, his projects with directors from Rajiv Rai and Aditya Chopra to Milan Luthria, Joy Augustine and others. Many of these figures were born after Bakshi began working in 1957!

Today, I can also say that most 're-creations' (a deplorable trend that indicates creative poverty and yet highlights the perennial quality of the originals) are made with Bakshi's songs: 'Main Jat Yamla Pagla Deewana', 'Mehbooba O Mehbooba', 'O Meri Mehbooba',

'Aa Dekhen Zara', 'Dum Maro Dum', 'Paisa Yeh Paisa', 'Tera Beemar Mera Dil', 'Ek Hasina Thi', 'Taiyab Ali', 'Tu Cheez Badi Hai Mast Mast', 'Aankh Maare', 'Tip Tip Barsa Pani' and many more. Such songs show us that his words have an instant resonance with GenY and GenZ. Thus, even youngsters can instantly identify with the typical Anand Bakshi song, due to the sentiments expressed in them.

Bakshi was also instrumental in the success of some of India's biggest composers, including R.D. Burman and Laxmikant–Pyarelal. Every hit or immortal song, as we all know, has a reason to become so. And that reason begins with the words . . .

The older folks have already experienced the magic of Bakshi's words. Many now realize that even the seemingly lighter Bakshi songs, which they merely enjoyed back in the day, can have deep insights— into character, situation and life itself. Like the *Nastik* song, '*Aaj ka yeh din kal ban jayega kal, peeche mudke na dekh pyaare aage chal.*'

That's what Bakshi's songs teach us—to live in the present and in sync with the times, with happiness as a *choice*. Remember his classic from the film *Amrit*, '*Duniya mein kitna gham hai / Mera gham itna kam hai / Logon ka gham dekha to / Main apna gham bhool gaya.*'

As long as Hindi film music lives on, Bakshi too will remain relevant. And he is among the *main* reasons why Hindi film music will survive for all time!

Manek Premchand (author and film historian)

Situational Imperative

It is strange how our minds work, isn't it? Often with leaps of associations. I live in Bombay, which is a wonderful city on many counts. But it has a few downsides, one of them being the presence of beggars at every street and traffic intersection. Whenever I see those beggars, I think of a popular joke that has done the rounds, and then with a quiet chuckle I think of the prodigious songwriter

Anand Bakshi. You have probably heard the joke before, but here it is anyway, followed by the reason why I think of Anand Bakshi in this context.

A beggar has been asking for alms on a busy street. A passer-by asks him how much money he wants. The beggar says Rs 20 would be nice. The man asks the beggar, 'Why do you need the money? To do drugs or to smoke?'

'Saahab, I don't do drugs or smoke.'

'What then? Booze?'

'I don't do any of these things. I'm just trying to eat and survive. *Main shareef aadmi hoon, ye sab naheen karta.*'

The man says, 'Okay, I'll tell you what. I won't give you Rs 20. I'll give you Rs 100 instead. But for that you'll have to come with me to my home, it's nearby.'

The beggar agrees. The householder rings the bell at his door. His wife opens it, and he tells her to look at this person, a *shareef aadmi* brought to beggary because he doesn't drink or smoke, the things that she keeps advising him against. The man gives the money to the beggar, shuts the door and tells his wife, 'This is what happens to people if they lead such a boring life.'

Joke done, my imagination now enters the scene. Now that a justification has been found, the householder pours himself a drink. Once under the influence, he starts singing the situational song 'Shareefon ka zamaane mein aji bas haal wo dekha ke sharaafat chhod di maine', originally sung by Lata Mangeshkar for Laxmikant–Pyarelal in *Sharafat* (1970). The lyrics were written by Anand Bakshi.

That was on a lighter note. On a more serious note, do consider the magnificence of this gifted writer who wrote songs so pertinent to the situations in films.

In *Zindagi Zindagi* (1972), the song 'Tu Ne Humein Kya Diya Ri Zindagi' is rendered by Kishore Kumar for S.D. Burman. Here, the writer addresses life itself and bemoans what it had done to him. It was the character Deb Mukerji, a patient, who sang this as he lay bedridden in the general ward of a hospital. The camera pans over Farida Jalal, Waheeda Rehman, Sunil Dutt and a slew of other patients, all of them clearly feeling the lyrics as they battled with the gloom of their individual destinies.

Anand Bakshi is remembered for his exceptional lyrics. Consider the qawwali pitting women against men in *Jabse Tumhen Dekha Hai* (1963). '*Tumhen husn deke Khuda ne sitamgar banaaya banaaya*' sing the men, led by Shammi Kapoor and Shashi Kapoor. But this line becomes a terrible opening gambit, backfiring on the men. The women, led by Shyama and Kumkum, respond with the killer line: '*Chalo is bahaane tumhen bhi Khuda yaad aaya ji aaya.*' The singers were Rafi, Manna Dey, Lata and Asha, in a studio presided over by the maestro Dattaram.

Bakshi wrote scores of situationally relevant songs, like 'Humein Kya Jo Harsu Ujaale Hue Hain' (Rafi/G.S. Kohli/*Namaste Ji*, 1965), 'Saawan Ka Maheena Pawan Kare Sor' (Mukesh, Lata/Laxmikant–Pyarelal/*Milan*, 1967), 'Kaahe Ko Roye' (S.D. Burman/S.D. Burman/*Aradhana*, 1969), 'Khilona Jaan Kar Tum Toh' (Rafi/Laxmi–Pyare/*Khilona*, 1970), 'Muhabbat Ke Suhaane Din' (Rafi/Kalyanji–Anandji/*Maryada*, 1971), 'Maar Diya Jaaye Ya Chhod Diya Jaaye' (Lata/Laxmi–Pyare/*Mera Gaon Mera Desh*, 1971) and 'Mujhko Hui Na Khabar' (Asha/Uttam Singh/*Dil Toh Pagal Hai*, 1997).

But perhaps the ultimate words that came out of Bakshi's mind were used for the many songs he wrote for *Amar Prem* (1971), which has music by R.D. Burman. In the Kishore Kumar song 'Kuchh Toh Log Kahenge', Rajesh Khanna attempts to console Sharmila Tagore, who is playing the role of a prostitute trapped in her destiny. Bakshi's lyrics in this song are transcendental and yet grounded in social reality. He has drawn from universal truths and from the Ramayana to come up with words that are situationally valid not just for a character in a film, but for all of us, carrying our own cross, crying about our own condition and looking for inspiration to somehow plod on and survive.

Kuchh to log kahenge, logon ka kaam hai kehna . . .
Kuchh reet jagat ki aisi hai, har ek subah ki shaam hui,
Tu kaun hai, tera naam hai kya, Sita bhi yahaan badnaam hui.
Phir kyoon sansaar ki baaton se bheeg gaye tere naina?

Words to frame in gold.

Thank you, Anand Bakshiji. You have enriched our lives with such wonderful poetry!

Acknowledgements

I would like to thank my brother, Gogi, for being like a parent to me after my parents departed; and my two sisters, Pappi and Rani, two more pillars of support through our lives. We are grateful for the affection and support we receive from Nidhi, Rohit, Nysa, Aditya, Chandni, Kahil, Divya, Karan, Shreya, Sidhant, Vinay Datt and Sanjiv Bali.

This effort of over nineteen years is my way to repay the debt of gratitude I owe my daddy for everything I got from him and for the inspiration that I, and millions of others, continue to derive from his lyrics. I was not the best of sons, so this book and the website www.anandbakshi.com are my tiny tributes to Daddy and my way of repaying him for everything he did for us. Daddy would tell us kids, 'Meri Maa ji ka pyar, phoolon ki chaaon thi.' For all of us, Daddy's love was the serene shade of flowers.

This memoir is thanks to my family, close friends and particularly his fans, whose love keeps his lyrics and songs alive. Thanks to Vinay Prajapati, who gifted us his domain name for our website. The book is also dedicated to his friend, the unsung hero, poet and editor Bismil Saeedi (from Tonk and Delhi), who nurtured Anand Bakshi in writing shayari; and to another unsung hero and dear friend of his, the Western Railway ticket collector Chhitar Mal Swaroop. Last but not least, to my mother, Kamla Mohan Bakhshi, who was the tallest pillar of his personal and professional life and of our family.

I owe a debt of gratitude to many more: Dad's friend and film-maker Subhash Ghai; my cousins Anita Datt Chopra and poet Neera Bakshi, and their mother, Shubh Khem Datt, for their memories; writer and photographer Shiraz Hassan and Waseem Altaf from Pakistan, for photographs of his Rawalpindi house, which still exists; our family's man Friday, Rajendra Bangera, for putting together various documents and images we needed for this memoir; Yunus Khan, Sheeba Lateef, Zohra Javed, Maria and Umar Riaz, for translating some Urdu poems/letters; Sushrut Mankad, for translating the Gujarati correspondence; the late Bhai Madan Mohan Singh Chhibber, for translating from the Urdu; the passionate writer and living legend Ali Peter John; lyricist Sameer Anjaan, for his affection.

And Anand Bakshi's passionate fans: lyricist Vijay Akela; Devmani Pandey; Paddy from Spotify; renowned film song historians and authors Dr Rajiv M. Vijayakar and Manek Premchand; poet and friend Harminder Singh Chawla; Vikas Manhas; editor Ganga Sharan Singh; radio presenter Yunus Khan for the Hindi translations; Rakesh Modi, Sangeeta Yadav; Anand Desai; Chandu Bardanwala; Hem Chand; poet Manohar Mohabbat Iyer; Ajay Poundarik; Aditya Pant; Gopal Patwal and Rashna Pochkhanawala from Saregama, who represents Anand Bakshi's maximum works as publisher; Jataneel Banerjee from Performing Right Society, UK; Rakesh Nigam, Manish Jani, Rumpa Banerjee from Indian Performing Right Society. And many others, some for their guidance, some for their knowledge, some for their encouragement and innumerable others for singing his lyrics and keeping our songs and creators alive. Poet Kishwari Jaipuri (Hasrat Sa'ab's daughter), for ensuring the translations from Urdu to English were correct and doing this for the bond of affection that Anand Bakshi and Hasrat Sa'ab shared.

My friend, writer and editor Shantanu Ray Chaudhuri, who has been motivating me since 2013 and who sowed the seeds for this book; senior commissioning editor Gurveen Chadha and editor Vineet Gill of Penguin Random House India, for reviewing my thoughts, revising my manuscript and turning it into a published book, as well as for their enthusiasm for the subject; editors complete and complement us authors. Rachna Pratap, for the friendly manner in which she negotiates contracts, always willing to explain and discuss terms authors like me find difficult to comprehend. Ahlawat Gunjan (and Jitesh Pillai, editor, *Filmfare*), for the gorgeous cover, and Akangksha Sarmah, for her beautiful design and aesthetic sense.

Our lives would not have been wholesome or complete without these friends and companions: Raghu, Harsh, Paramjit, Veena, buddy Rohit, buddy Swami, Jayanthi, buddy Ambiii, Raman, Satya, Ritu, Shomieee, Maneck, Dilnaz, Dinyar, Tony, Anupama, Sonu, Priyanka, Meghna, Benaifer, Khusrav, Siddhi, buddy Kanika, Akira, Priyanka, Abhay, Rishi, Shashi, Pooja, Changez, Shyam, Mayura, Vivek, Ankita, Himanshu, Manoj, Vidyut, Akshita, Nishil, Ayesha, Sydney, Annalise, Dr Apte, Amin, Charlotte, Dr Ishani, Bobby, Amit, Rohan, Vidyun, Tony, Meenu, Sushrut, Bhavesh, Rustom, Nandu, Sharad, Saqib, Sabeena, Shachi, Sumant, Babbuji and Vimala. If I have missed out on any names of the precious people who have contributed so kindly to this book and to my life, sorry, please excuse me for it.

A massive thanks to *Reader's Digest*—a wonderful magazine that inspired my father and has inspired me for nearly half my life. And thanks to the Swedish actress Ingrid Bergman. I read her biography in 2002, and it reinforced my passion and love for biographies, writing, film-making and cinema. Thanks also to the wonderful Internet and its vast resources. What would our lives be without it!

This memoir is dedicated to all who refuse to give up on their dreams and ambitions, even when no one supports them. Anand Bakshi's life was evidence that you only need one person to believe in your dreams, and that person is YOU. It's a tribute to people who move to alien lands to chase their single-minded goals, as Bakhshi had arrived decades ago on the shores of Bambai.

Before we part, I can say with conviction: Have faith in God, the universe, your destiny, your deeds, your choices, luck, family and yourself. You will need a little bit of all that now and then. Most importantly, be grateful, stay inspired, inspire others, stay loved and love yourself too. I hope to travel with you again, with some other *kisse*, *baatein* and *yaadein* soon. *Shukriya*.

Rakesh Anand Bakshi